THE DESERT

THE DESERT

❖ ❖ ❖ *Le Désert*

Pierre Loti

TRANSLATED BY Jay Paul Minn

UNIVERSITY OF UTAH PRESS
Salt Lake City

∞ Printed on acid-free paper

This translation is based on the 1896 Calmann Lévy edition of *Le Désert*.

LIBRARY OF CONGRESS CATALOGING-IN-PUBLICATION DATA

Loti, Pierre, 1850–1923.
    [Désert. English]
    The desert / Pierre Loti ; translated by Jay Paul Minn.
       p.   cm.
    ISBN 0-87480-427-2
    1. Loti, Pierre, 1850–1923—Journeys—Egypt—Sinai. 2. French—
Travel—Egypt—Sinai—History—19th century. 3. Novelists, French—
19th century—Biography. 4. Deserts—Egypt—Sinai. 5. Camels—Egypt—
Sinai. I. Title.
PQ2472.Z5A8923   1993
848'.803—dc20   93-10090
[B]   CIP

❖❖❖   TRANSLATOR'S ACKNOWLEDGMENTS

I AM DEEPLY INDEBTED to my wife, Niki, for her constant support and advice during this fascinating project. My thanks also to our friends and colleagues: Robert Ariew, for his encouragement and help with the Word; to Ingeborg Kohn, for the Consideration; and to Peter Wild, for the Idea. I am especially grateful to the University of Utah Press and Jeff Grathwohl for their trust and respect.

Jay Paul Minn
Professor Emeritus
Knox College

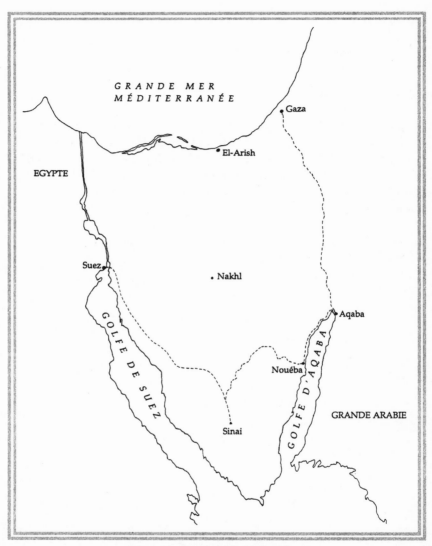

Pierre Loti's Travels in the Sinai

Eccentric! Decadent! The words are pale when applied to Pierre Loti, the pseudonym of Julien Viaud, 1850–1923. A simple biographical list can only hint at his range of talent and genius, and one wonders how this extraordinary individual with all his debauchery (consorting with countesses, the queen of Romania, and an internationally famous actress, among other attachments) could rise to the top of the literary heap and be recognized throughout the world as a great writer.

His sexual excesses and experimentation, however, reflect the Decadent movement of his time, fitting nicely in temperament and kind with the exploits of other great contemporary French writers such as Rimbaud and Verlaine.

The Decadent movement in France at the end of the nineteenth century blended with the Symbolist (Impressionist) movement, what we might call "hippiedom" today. Dedicated to excesses of all kinds, these very creative people loved to engage in the odd, the new, the different; often their purpose was not simply personal pleasure, but also to "titillate the middle class," *épater les bourgeois*.

Loti was born late in the life of his parents, and he was frustratingly separated in age from his siblings by many years. The family was Protestant in Catholic France, another challenge for this Frenchman from Rochefort, in the provinces. He was very short, and all his siblings were tall; this bothered him deeply all his life. He wrote novels that endeared him to an international public and made him rich (*My Brother Ives, Icelandic Fisherman, Aziyadé,* and *Madame Chrysanthemum* being the most popular). He was an artist whose drawings are technically brilliant and whose perception of color was exquisitely tuned. He was an officer in the French navy and managed to see the ports of the United States, China, and

South America, to mention just a few. Deciding that he needed to be stronger physically, possibly in an attempt to compensate for his short stature, he took a year's leave from the French navy and developed such a fine physique that he joined a circus as an acrobat.

He and his wife had one son. But Loti decided that the lineage of his family was not sturdy enough, so he advertised through his lawyer for a young Basque woman willing to give up her family and home and to live in Loti's neighborhood and bear his children. After a diligent search, such a woman was found. Loti supported her in comfort, and she bore him two sons, whom he acknowledged as his own.

His sexual prowess hints strongly at bisexuality, although solid proof of the male side is lacking. However, he did have deep emotional attachments to several men. Biographers assume that he was trying to replace an older brother who had been like a father to him and who had drowned tragically at sea. Loti never recovered emotionally from this loss.

Loti loved to wear disguises. And as he became more affluent, he threw exotic parties, where everyone had to wear costumes matching the theme of the party. As he fell under the spell of new cultures, he converted the decor of his home, room by room, to reflect such styles as Moroccan, Chinese, and Japanese. For these rooms he imported, at great expense, authentic and rich furnishings from the original countries.

Even when in the navy, he wore makeup, sometimes in excess. One commander recommended that this man never be promoted because he wore too much. But another commander later recommended promotion, in spite of the makeup, insisting that he was an extremely competent officer.

The men on his ships adored him. Knowing that he was a lover of cats, and seeing that he had picked up a stray kitten when they were anchored at Tripoli, his men once threw an elaborate onboard christening ceremony for the cat, to make it a proper Christian! This sort of fun hit the Paris newspapers. Imagine, a provincial Protestant French naval officer who mocked a holy sacrament on a French ship!

He was taken into the French Academy, one of the highest honors France can give, as an acknowledgment of his novels and renown. He had many devoted friends, but the closest and most loyal was the great actress Sarah Bernhardt. They spent many hours together talking about literature, art, and spirituality; he confirms that in her bedroom she had a satin-lined coffin, where she slept when depressed. She came to him on short notice as a supportive friend when he had serious problems to resolve. They both died in 1923.

The Desert ("A Quest in 1894")

First published in Paris by Calmann-Lévy in 1895, this book has had a phenomenal appeal in French through dozens of editions. Indeed the book's international influence had a large impact on an entire genre of writing in the United States. Loti's lush prose probably served as a prime model for John C. Van Dyke's *The Desert* (1901), the first book to praise the arid lands of the American Southwest. In turn Van Dyke's volume became the grandfather of almost all American desert writing.

Loti's book is a diary that he kept as he went from Suez to Jerusalem on camelback through the Sinai deserts. He describes in detail the various sheiks he met and the organization of the caravan, all crafted with poetic prose of gripping visual beauty. He is especially talented at descriptions of the natural surroundings, both awesome and terrifying. His refined attention to gradations of color are those of a gifted painter and poet. But the personal opinions and decisions revealed as the work proceeds show us a complex person of great expressive power.

His author's preface hints at the reason for the trip: Loti had become an atheist. He had been especially attracted to Islam and expressed intentions to convert. His mother, a devout Huguenot, argued that the Christian heaven is separate from the Moslem heaven; consequently he and she would be separated for eternity. Although he capitulated to his mother's wish in this matter, he obviously had difficulty recovering his Christian faith and was permanently mesmerized by Islam.

In an attempt to recover his faith, Loti decided to visit the Holy Land, but not the easy way by sea. Instead he chose the hardships and perils of the open desert. But one can easily see that he made the trip in relative luxury and comfort. He had two traveling companions: the *handsome* (as he was called) Léo Thémèze and the duke of Talleyrand-Périgord. There were at least twenty camels in the caravan, loaded down with water, food, and amenities such as tents, Persian rugs, furniture, and servants. He thought that by suffering (as he saw it) in the desert he would prepare his soul for Jerusalem and a reawakening of his faith.

The book takes on a religious tone, almost frantic in its intensity. Not only does Loti quote from the Bible, he also sees the desert as primordial, taking his imagination back not only to biblical times but also beyond. In addition he elevates certain exotic people to religious status; a monk at Saint Catherine's Monastery seems Christ reborn to him, while ghosts and phantoms abound. And he chastises the people in Gaza for not displaying more Christianity on Easter Sunday. Even clouds and the myriad facets of nature are often described as "mysterious," enhancing the tone of religious quest that is the essential substance of the book. Many sentences start with the conjunction "and," a very common feature of the King James Bible and of Arabic texts (Loti spoke Arabic and Turkish fluently), lending a deep religious and literary air to the whole text.

There is also considerable historical information of interest to students of the Sinai and Holy Land. Some of the sheiks he met in 1894, for example, are the ancestors of more contemporary rulers, and it is fascinating to see how these people governed. Loti claims in his author's preface that there will be no frightening things in his book; but he more than adequately describes several occasions or moods which do lend an air of fright. He faces these events with a macho attitude of "full speed ahead," no matter what danger might present itself.

However, his tender side reveals him to be an early sympathizer with animal rights, as shown by his touching reaction to the death of an owl and its solemn burial in the sand.

The Desert takes Loti to Gaza and is volume one of a trilogy. The following two books are *Jerusalem* and *Galilee*. Some critical thought places Loti's travel books in a higher category than his novels, partly because the travel books are free from the sometimes melodramatic plots of his novels; however, this takes nothing away from the powerful prose of the novels. It is also proposed that the unity of *Le Désert* with biblical texts gives it an aura uncommon in the literature.

The Translation

Loti's prose covers a wide range of styles, depending on his intentions in any given context. Already mentioned is his frequent use of "and," particularly at the beginning of sentences that often do not fit together logically. This enhances the work's poetry. The book is often abrupt in style, containing phrases without verbs, consistent with the telegraphic jotting of detail in a diary, but often beautifully poetic in the turn of phrase.

Many paragraphs are quite long, held together by a basic thought or picture, with sentences and phrases joined by semicolons. Some of these have been broken up into independent sentences or phrases for easier reading, without, it is hoped, diminishing the impact of this powerful prose.

Rhythms and sequences of vowels and consonants have been carefully chosen, to preserve as much poetry as possible from the original text. At times the rhythm demands one syllable for a word and then might require two syllables later on for the same word.

Thus, sometimes a different English word will translate the same French word in different contexts. The best example perhaps is the French word *désert,* which does not necessarily equate with *desert* in English. Thus its translation can range in syllables from one to three, from *wastes*, through *wasteland / desert,* to *wilderness*, that is, uninhabited land.

Loti's frequent use of demonstrative adjectives ("this," "those," etc.) and adverbs of place ("here," "there") gives an immediacy to his descriptions. Also, in keeping with the flavor of his time, some proper names have been retained in the original because of the charming French spelling Loti gave them. For example, he calls an outpost "N'Nouébia," whereas several maps give "Nuweiba"; likewise with "Wady," which he spells "Ouady"; and "Djebel-Tih" is more appealing than "Gebel-Tih." Also preserved are most of Loti's quaint spellings of Turkish and Arabic words and phrases. Loti's versions seem more colorful, adding to the nostalgia and poetry of the whole book. And immediacy is further enhanced by his frequent use of the historical present tense. It is as if we are there with him.

Above all this first English translation of this influential book is an attempt to convey the serious, if unusual and at times fervent, search of Loti for his Final Answer. This beautiful work reveals to us a rudderless man retracing biblical trails in the wilderness. Loti had the talent and the vision to convey his attempt to recover his faith in a manner that places his work among the finest of the nineteenth century.

We are fortunate that he cared to show us his world enough and time. All the while in his quest he is standing seemly human and exceeding tall.

Jay Paul Minn
Peter Wild

WHERE ARE MY DREAM brothers, those who were kind enough to follow me into the asphodel fields of dark Maghreb on the Moroccan plains? . . . May those, but only they, come with me to Petraean Arabia and its vast echoing desert.

And may they know in advance that there will be in this book neither terrible adventures, nor extraordinary chases, nor discoveries, nor dangers. No, nothing but the fantasy of a slow journey, at the pace of swaying camels in the infinite of the pink desert.

Then, after the long road fret with mirages, Jerusalem will appear, or at least its great shadow. And then perhaps, oh my dream brothers, in doubt and anguish we will prostrate ourselves together there, in the dust, before inexpressible ghosts.

Pierre Loti

ONE

❖ ❖ ❖ *The Moses Oasis, February 22, 1894*

Through the mercy of Allah most high, this document
comes from Allah's most humble and devoted servant the
Seïd Omar, son of Edriss, for the intention of his friend
Pierre Loti, as a recommendation to the chiefs of all the
Arabian tribes to elicit aid and respect during his trip
through Arab lands, for he venerates Islam and is
motivated by the best feelings for our religion.

And I will be pleased with all those who have
respected and assisted him, for he is worthy.

Written by us, Chaban 10, 1311,
Omar, Son of Edriss, El Senoussi El Hosni

Now that I have been in my tent at the desert's edge for an
hour, I am rereading this letter, which is to be my safe-conduct
through hostile tribes. At the bottom of the page, mysterious characters spell out the inscrutable divine invocation of the Senoussite
sect; this group has its seat over in the Maghreb and its Seïd is the
representative for Eastern Arabia.

I don't believe the trip is really dangerous, so the strange attraction of danger is not what brings me to this land. Men and things of
our century have brought their godlessness here; but my purpose is
to prepare my spirit with the slow healing power of the wilderness
on my way along old abandoned trails to Holy Jerusalem.

Several trails in the sand were offered to me.

First of all, the easiest and shortest, the one called "The Little
Desert," by way of El-Arish and the shores of the Egyptian gulf.
Alas, it has already been ruined over the years by a flood of idle

Englishmen and Americans, whose comfort and protection have been provided by special agencies.

Or the second, a less traveled one, through the Sinai and Nakhl.

Or the third and longest of all, through the Sinai, Aqaba, and the Petraean desert. I chose this one because the guides kept advising against it. This route is harder in all respects, and Egyptians consider it bad at the present time, due to the rebellion of the Idumean tribes. And for ten years no European has tried to use it. The Sheik of Petra especially was described to me as a dangerous caravan predator, currently independent of any recognized government, but he himself attracts me in his direction more than his country does. Moreover, he is affiliated with the Senoussite sect, as are almost all the chiefs of the Idumea and the Hidjaz; no doubt for him alone will I need the Seïd Omar's letter.

The first disappointment of my journey is the world of difference between the distinguished Seïd and my escort of cowed, servile Bedouin. But the desert does not disappoint, even here at this threshold where it is just beginning to appear. Its immensity overwhelms everything, enlarges everything, and in its presence the wickedness of human beings is forgotten.

And how quickly we have been taken prisoner by it! How suddenly have we been wrapped in silence and solitude! . . . Just yesterday morning we were in Cairo bursting with tourists, its life so much like any elegant winter haven. Yesterday evening it was Suez, already more isolated, in a shabby little hotel that smelled of colony and sand. Today, after our farewells to the last Europeans, the boat brought us in a stiff wind from the west coast of the Red Sea, and put us ashore on a deserted beach. Nobody and nothing anymore, as the desolate night descended . . .

❖ ❖ ❖

HOWEVER, PEOPLE OUT THERE were watching us from behind the slender palms of the Moses Oasis, which was a distant dark spot on the expanse of sand. And coming toward us we saw camels on the run, driven by scruffy-looking Bedouin.

The camel drivers smiled as they came closer, and we could see that they were part of our group and their beasts were to be our mounts. The men were armed with daggers and long iron cutlasses. Their dried-up mummy bodies could be glimpsed through openings in the incredible rags they were wearing, tatters of goatskin and shreds of burnous. They were shivering in the cheerless evening wind, and their smiles exposed long teeth.

In half an hour, they led us to the Moses Spring Oasis, our first stop for the desert trails. Our tents, which had left Cairo two days before us, were already set up among the slender palms. Our interpreter and servants, all Arabs from Syria, were waiting for us. And around the camp our twenty camel drivers with our twenty camels were a mass of animal wretchedness and ugliness, men and beasts lying together on the sand reeking with their urine and dung.

Near us another caravan, larger than ours but less well equipped, was sprawled out on the ground in the same kind of profusion. They were Russian pilgrims, priests, peasants, and weary old women—all people of burning faith on their way back from the Sinai with deep coughs and haggard faces, after so many days of sun and so many nights of freezing air.

And suddenly all around us there was infinite emptiness, the desert at twilight, swept by a steady cold wind: the desert of a neutral and dead color, spreading under a darker sky that seemed to fall and crush it out to the edges of the horizon all around.

Then, after taking this in, we were overcome with a strange intoxicating shiver of solitude: a need to feel more alone, an irrational need, a physical desire to run in the wind to the nearest high ground, in order to see farther, farther into the compelling immensity . . .

From the top of the desolate dune where this path took us, you could in fact see farther, and on the desert thus enlarged there was a last lingering gleam of daylight, coming down from the yellow sky through a rip that was slowly forming in its veil . . .

This winter wind whipped everything up, and it became so threatening that we felt a sadness of ancestral and distant origin, a melancholy that was suddenly combined with the attraction of vastness, regret for having come, and a temptation to retreat, something like the instinctive fear that makes the animals of green lands turn back when they see such regions, where death hovers in wait.

❖ ❖ ❖

ISOLATED IN THE TENT from wind and light for our first nomad dinner, we were struck with carefree levity, set against this great mute threshold where twilight was ending.

And then there was the very childish fun of putting on our Arab outfits—new for my two traveling companions but not for me. Rather unnecessary these disguises, it is true, especially in this first part of the Sinai desert, where so many Europeans have already passed. But the clothes are more suitable for the burning sun of the days as well as for the cold of the nights. Above all it is unquestionably more appropriate clothing for traveling by camel. When one is not alone, one owes it to others not to flaunt the ridiculous blotch of an English outfit in a desert painting, and it is almost a question of protocol toward one's neighbor to blend as an artist might.

So for many days we will not wear our western jackets. We'll be unfettered and perhaps more dashing in long burnouses and veils—like Arabian sheiks. And we are impatiently looking forward to our early start tomorrow morning.

TWO

> So Moses brought Israel from the Red sea, and they went
> out into the wilderness of Shur; and they went three days
> in the wilderness, and found no water.
>
> (*Exodus* xv:22)

THE WATER OF THE Nile follows us to the Shur desert in barrels and leather bottles. All day long, plodding in the enormity of arid sand, we follow the worn imprints left infrequently by man and beast through the centuries; these are the desert roads . . . Far off, the monotonous horizons tremble. Sands sown with grayish stones, all in shades of pink-gray and yellow-gray. From time to time, a pale green plant with a barely noticeable black flower—and the long necks of the camels bend down, stretch, and try to graze.

The horizons shimmer with heat. At times you hope to shade your head under a wayward cloud in the endless sky. The cloud casts a shadow that wanders like us along the infinite sands. But it passes and disappears. These ineffective little shadows scoot away, cooling only stones or old whitened bones.

Useless also are the thicker clouds that, moving now from bright morning to midday, are beginning to pile up over there on the dead mountains. The clouds are bringing their veil of coolness and mystery to a place where nothing exists. More and more they condense, covering those distant lifeless places with a foggy haze.

Change and the unreal seem to surround us now. The sand we are approaching is drowning everywhere in an ever-darker sky, and finally the sun itself darkens as if to die. Here and there those chaotic dark curtains tear open and the barren summit of a mountain

5

brightens. Or under a breach shedding rays of light, a mica-carpeted sand dune begins to shine nearby like a silver sepulchral mound.

During the dull halt of midday, our baggage camels pass us, as is usual in a caravan. They are carrying our tents and things away into the forbidding distance, so that we can find our camp set up when we arrive at nightfall.

So with a smaller group we continue the last trek of the day. And little by little your mind is put to sleep by the hypnotic slow rocking of the great tireless beast as it goes along, goes along on its long legs. And in the nearest level of the gray that surrounds you, your eyes are dimmed with sleep and staring down. All you see is the continual swaying of his neck, the same yellow-gray color as the sand, and the back of his hairy head, like a little lion's head, surrounded with white shells and blue beads set in pendants of black wool.

❖ ❖ ❖

TOWARD EVENING WE ENTER an area sown with spindly bushes as far as the eye can see; a kind of shabby garden with no visible limits— and the rising wind covers and clouds it over with a fine dust of sand.

Ever stronger is the invincible wind. In the dying light, things can now be seen only through the startling transparency of this strange yellow cloud. And our tents, appearing and growing larger as we approach, take on the dimensions of pyramids in the naked emptiness of this sandy blur—and our baggage camels wander around grazing on broom, and seem to be enormous beasts that could eat trees, in the dying pale light of the setting sun.

As the wind rises and shakes our tents with the racket of a sea vessel's sails, we stop for the night, in this forlorn spot, in this endless solitude.

THREE

❖ ❖ ❖   *Saturday, February 24*

Until two in the morning, the wind has been steadily attacking our little camp, lost in this empty place. Our tents flap with the whooshing of canvas. In the dark you can feel cloths trembling overhead. My light cot is shaken, as if at sea in rough weather, and around the camp our camels all complain like zoo animals. In spite of yourself, you think how vulnerable our portable canvas houses would be against the night forces and whatever surprises the desert might bring. With so much noise and so many quaverings in the dark, hands could be on you, a blade against your throat, without your having heard anything, without your fellow travelers in nearby tents suspecting anything.

❖ ❖ ❖

At sunrise the weather has become calm and still. Then you look around as you get out of the tent. The sun is rising in an absolutely pure sky. No trace of last night's weirdness. Things have regained their true proportion of real camels, sand, and spindly brush. Everything is sharp, as if frozen in an unearthly harsh light, and above the lapis sheet of the Red Sea, the distant mountains of Egypt can still be dimly seen.

All morning long, ambling, ambling in the wilderness, at the same slow and steady pace. The plants are thinning out. Here and there comes a strange, solitary sand flower, a leafless sheath colored yellow and violet standing out of the soil.

And nothing living anywhere: no beast, no bird, no insect. Even the world-traveler fly does not exist here. While the wastelands of the sea revitalize the riches of life, here is nothing but sterility and death. And you are overwhelmed with silence and nonlife, in the midst of vigorous pristine air as virginal as before the world was.

The sun rises, burns, and spreads its increasingly hypnotic white fire. On the ground there are scatterings of little black pebbles or sparklings of mica. But no plants now, nothing anymore.

And the terrain begins to get rough, almost mountainous: piles of gravel and stones, forever useless and unusable, taking on (one wonders why and for whose eyes) very odd shapes that have been unchanged for centuries in this same silence and these same splendors of light. Against the dazzling sunlight you close your eyes in spite of yourself for very long intervals; when you open them again, the harsh horizon seems a black circle slashing the brilliant sky; but where you happen to be is astonishingly white, with the shadows of our big plodding animals skipping over silvery bits of mica as we sway endlessly to and fro.

Toward evening we approach an area of high ground. And at the depressing time when the winter sun stretches our shadows enormously in our great sand and stone amphitheater, the mountains before us display a marvelous range of colors: iris-violet at the bottom, shades of peony-pink at the summits, the whole thing set against a pale greenish sky.

Longer and longer are the shadows of things, even the smallest dunes and smallest stones. And our shadows on the sand are almost infinite; we seem to be riding camels on stilts, apocalyptic beasts with long ibis legs.

But night is falling and we don't see our camp. How endless the trip is today!

❖ ❖ ❖

NIGHT HAS NOW FALLEN, although the mountains in the distance still shine reddish, as if smoldering from a glowing fire. And we on the other hand are in the blackness of forbidding little valleys, stripped of all life. Our camels can't see well and complain, not knowing where to set down their big hesitant hooves.

Where will our tents be tonight? Our guide seems to be lost, and a vague concern overtakes us in this limitless isolation.

Finally, finally, going around a hill: fires! yellow flames dancing ahead! As we arrive our Bedouin come to meet us with lanterns. They have set up our camp this time in a carefully chosen place, butted against a wall of rocks that give the illusion of protection against nighttime surprises. And one feels a deeper impression of home upon entering canvas houses where torches are ablaze. With their embroidered arabesques and their oriental rugs on the ground, the tents seem like little nomad palaces to our eyes, which were already mesmerized by the neutral tones of nothing at all.

However, yesterday's cold wind has come up, apparently as it will every night, and which is like the breathing of the desert. It is starting to shake the canvas of our frail temporary abodes, in the desolation and night that hem us in everywhere.

And some men have come out of the supposedly protective rocks. There they are, strangers, with black faces and white teeth, prowling in the dark beyond our fires.

FOUR

❖❖❖ *Sunday, February 25*

A T THE SPLENDID SUNRISE, our camp awakens, stirs, and regroups
for setting off. Above the broad rock wall behind us stands the
white moon, watching us leave with its dying light in the blue sky.

First off and until broiling noon, the wastes are sown with
black pebbles, as if covered with coal dust. These pebbles shine and
sparkle under blistering sunlight, creating a watery mirage for
thirsty passersby. We plod on for hours through the black wilderness, full of glistenings. In spots, streaks of saltpeter and salts marble the sand with gray. Nothing sings, nothing flies, nothing moves.
But the enormous silence is pummeled into deeper silence by the
incessant, monotonous clump-clump of our plodding camels . . .

Toward noon an area less dead. At the edge of what looks like a
dried-up streambed, there are colorless tamarinds growing and pale
bushes covered with little white flowers—and even two tall palms.

A startled gray swallow swoops by. And flies reappear around
the tearing eyes of our camels. Some attempt at life! And two big
black birds, masters of this place, spread their wings and screech off
into the silence.

Upon seeing the palm trees, our Bedouin escorts sense that
there is water under their narrow shade and turn our animals that
way. Indeed, a little water has collected in a sandy depression, and
the camels, groaning joyously, push toward it, trying to stick their
muzzles into it, two and three at once, jumbling their long
stretched necks together.

Then the desert again, drier and more sterile. Going deeper
into the mountainous territories of the interior, we are still moving
away from the Red Sea, out of sight since yesterday. How many dismal valleys and great desolate arenas will we cross before our
evening rest!

Our camels keep going, going at the same hypnotic pace, following almost on their own the same barely visible desert paths that their ancestors followed and marked throughout the ages, going in this same direction, the only direction much used in the Sinai.

Toward evening three heavily veiled women go by on young camels with muzzles to the wind. A moment later a dark-skinned boy, who seems upset by their flight, follows them into the wasteland until we lose sight of them. His camel, decorated with embroidered shells, had fringes and pendants of black wool fluttering in the breeze of his run.

Mountains rise and valleys fall around us as the day wears on. The mountains are made of sand, clay, and white stones. They are a mass of primordial stuff, piled up in ragged geological formations, never disturbed by man, and slowly creased by rain, slowly crumbled by sun, ever since the beginning of the world. The formations take on the strangest shapes, and one could say that some hand has taken the trouble to arrange and group them, one after the other. For a league there are rows of cones, stacked and layered as if deliberately symmetrical. Then the peaks flatten out, and they become rows of cyclopean tables. Then come domes and cupolas, like the ruins of ancient cities. And you are overwhelmed by the wile and uselessness of these forms—as it all goes by in continual deathly silence under the same merciless light, always with brilliant sparkles of mica, spread out as if on a circus cape.

From time to time one of the camel drivers sings, and his voice draws us from our sluggishness and daydreams. His enormously sad song is just a series of supplicating cries, where the awesome name of Allah is the refrain—along the valley walls it stirs dormant vibrant echoes into almost terrifying tones.

❖ ❖ ❖

AT TWILIGHT, THE MOMENT when the magic of sunset comes down over the desert for us, we make camp in a huge, gloomy, nameless arena, composed completely of dirty gray clay and surrounded by a wall of enormous rocks. No water here. But we have enough water from the Nile for two or three days more, and our guide, the sheik, promises to have us camp at a spring tomorrow night.

As soon as our tents are set up, our camels, finding themselves freed from their heavy loads, wander around the camp looking for sparse broom. Our Arabs, who are seeking dry sticks for the camp fires, seem like witches in long robes collecting herbs for evil spells at nightfall. And for one night our little nomadic town gives the illusion of life in this forsaken place, where we will never again return and where deathly silence will again descend tomorrow.

The desolation here becomes steadily more awe-inspiring as the sun falls and flames out. An immense arena, seemingly surrounded by ruins of cities, chaotic things, bowled over, defoliated, and worked into fissures or caves. And, as with our camels, our Bedouin, the soil, and everything else, these are all in tints of ashes or burnt sienna that form the endless setting, the neutral but intensely hot setting. And over it all the desert unfurls and spreads its weird spectacle of light.

Now the time of sunset, the magic time. On the distant heights there appear the fleeting incandescent violets and glowing reds. It all seems to come from fire . . .

And now the sun is down; but, although everything is getting darker, a latent fire, a fire reluctant to die, smolders for a long time in the browns and ash-grays that are the true colors of things here . . . Then a shudder in the sky, and suddenly the cold comes down, the inevitable desert cold.

❖ ❖ ❖

WHEN NIGHT HAS COME, when the stars are aglow in the enormous sky, and when as usual our Bedouin have sat down around their fires of branches—black silhouettes against yellow sparks—a dozen of them break away and come to our tents, forming a circle around someone playing a small bagpipe, and they begin to sing together. In time with the slow tempo set by the musette player, they rock their heads as they sing. The tune is old and sad, no doubt much as it was when Moses was here. Sadder than silence is this Bedouin music, which rises suddenly to a roar and which seems to be lost in air unused to noise, air as thirsty for sound as this sand is thirsty for dew . . .

FIVE

❖ ❖ ❖ *Monday, February 26*

Every morning you wake up in a different setting of the vast desert. You leave your tent and are surrounded by the splendor of the virginal morning. You stretch your arms and half-naked body in the cold pure air. Out on the sand, you wrap your turban and drape yourself in your white woolen veils. You get drunk on light and space. At the time of waking, you know the heady intoxication of just being able to breathe, just being alive . . .

And then off you go, perched atop the ever-moving camel that steadily plods along until nighttime. You go along, go along, go along, and you see in front of you a hairy head decorated with shells and its long neck, cutting the air like the prow of a ship at sea. Wasteland follows wasteland. You stretch your ears into the silence and you hear nothing, not a birdsong, nor the buzz of a fly, because there is nothing alive anywhere . . .

After a chilly dawn, the sun suddenly climbs and warms. The four hours of our morning travel as we go east into the sun are the most dazzling time of the day. Then we have our noon stop at a randomly chosen spot, in a flimsy tent that was set up quickly. The slower caravan of our Bedouin and baggage camels catches up, goes by with shouts as if at a wild party, and disappears into the unknown ahead. Then, after the four hours of our afternoon trek, we finally arrive at our new place for the night, and we have the simple physical joy of finding our tents again, where our gentle dromedaries kneel to set us down.

❖ ❖ ❖

This morning we start off into hot valleys between claustrophobic mountains. The sun is dreary, dreary; it is like a big dying ember

that could fall from the sky. Your tired eyes follow the shadows of
the camels as they move along the reflecting sand. And as always
happens when you approach distant mountains, the mountains
seem black in contrast with the sheen of the sand nearby.

Toward afternoon we are very high up in the remote wastes of
the Sinai peninsula. New spaces unfold on all sides; this tangible
sign of their immensity increases our understanding of what
wilderness is, but it also intimidates us more.

And it is an almost terrifying magnificence . . . In a distance
that is much clearer than usual earthly distances, mountain chains
join and overlap. They are in regular arrangements that man has
not interfered with since the creation of the world. And they have
harsh brittle edges, never softened by the least vegetation. The closest row of mountains is a reddish brown; then, as they stand closer
to the horizon, the mountains go through elegant violet, turning a
deeper and deeper blue, until they are pure indigo in the farthest
chain. And everything is empty, silent, and dead. Here you have the
splendor of fixed perspectives, without the ephemeral attraction of
forests, greeneries, and grasslands; it is also the splendor of almost
eternal stuff, freed of life's instabilities. The geological splendor
from before the Creation . . .

❖ ❖ ❖

FROM ANOTHER HEIGHT at evening, we discover a plain with no visible limits, composed of sand and stone, speckled with spindly reddish bushes. The plain is flooded with light, burning with the sun's
rays, and our camp, already set up out there with its infinitely tiny
white tents, becomes a pygmy village dwarfed by this magnificent
wilderness.

❖ ❖ ❖

OH! THE SUNSET THIS TIME! Never had we seen so much gold spread
out around our lonely camp for us alone. And as our camels are

doing their usual evening foraging, they loom strangely large against the empty horizon and have gold on their heads, on their legs, and on their long necks. They are completely edged with gold. The plain is all gold. And the bushes are gold . . .

Then comes the night, the clear silent night . . .

And now you feel an almost religious fear if you wander away and lose sight of the camp. But in order to be absolutely alone in the black emptiness, you separate yourself from your little handfull of living things lost in this dead land. The stars shine in the cosmic void but are closer and more accessible than before. In this desert the stars are permanent and ageless; looking at them here, one feels closer to understanding their inconceivable infinity; one almost has the illusion of truly being united with universal permanence and time . . .

SIX

❖ ❖ ❖ *Tuesday, February 27*

> For they were departed from Rephidim, and were come to
> the desert of Sinai, and had pitched in the wilderness.
>
> (*Exodus* xix:2)

FIVE DAYS NOW WITHOUT finding water. But we still have enough
from the Nile.

Traveled all morning in yesterday's plain, where the broom has
been replaced with sparser clumps of plants, whitish green, half-
buried in sand, balls of thorns that could pierce feet like iron spikes.

We are beginning to come upon big black stones standing up-
right on the sand, set up like men or menhirs. At first rather sparse,
they become more and more numerous—and also taller and taller.
Then little by little, as we go on gently swaying, they take on the dimensions of dungeons, towers, and fortresses; finally they group,
forming corridors, like the streets of some destroyed cyclopean
city—and they enclose us with dark walls.

❖ ❖ ❖

THE NOON STOP IS IN one of these forbidding valleys . . .

While we are sleeping on our carpets, raucous loud voices suddenly resound from the reflecting stones. Our guards, our drivers,
and our camels are letting us know they are going by. It's the slower
caravan that follows us every morning and gets ahead of us during
our noon rest, so that it can beat us to the evening stop. Both animals and men usually greet us with shrieks as they go by, and today
their voices are more piercing, due to surprisingly loud echoes from
these dry rocks that resonate like dead wood.

❖ ❖ ❖

WE PROCEED UNTIL the hour of evening prayer through narrow winding valleys. But their walls are constantly changing shape and color. They become pink granite, veined with broad bands of blue or green rock.

This region is less desolate than before, because here we have trees, the first we have seen in five days. Oh, wretched little trees, a kind of thorny mimosa like those you find in the Sahara, in Senegal, and Obock; during this early spring they have just turned light green, with barely visible pale leaves. And strewn about occasionally among chunks of granite, there are delicate little white flowers.

At a fork in these valleys, we came upon two adorable Bedouin youngsters, brother and sister, who watched us approaching with fright in their dark velvet eyes. They tell us there are campsites up in the mountain. Indeed we hear distant guard dogs barking to announce our presence. Soon afterwards we see herds of goats shepherded by Bedouin dressed and veiled in black.

Our old driver-sheik then comes and requests my permission to leave us until tomorrow, so that he can visit this tribe, where he has sons.

❖ ❖ ❖

WE COME CLOSE TO the "Myrrh Mountain" and suddenly the whole desert has a delightful scent, because skinny little plants release delicious, strange odors as they are crushed by the hooves of our camels.

The ground of these interminable mountain passes is slowly climbing toward the central plateau in almost unnoticeable degrees. We will continue to go up for two more days, slowly heading for the Sinai Convent at a height of two thousand meters.

We are still in rough terrain. Very recently mountains must have crumbled, breaking up on the sand with apocalyptic noise, for gigantic ruins with fresh fractures give evidence of past catastro-

phes. And we continue our ascent on crumbled blue and pink granite, between stands of the same rock that are cracked at the bottom,
seemingly on the verge of tumbling down.

For the night we camp in a high valley beside stark and frightening embankments of red granite, where the air is turning cold as
ice.

SEVEN

> And it came to pass on the third day in the morning, that
> there were thunders and lightnings, and a thick cloud
> upon the mount, and the voice of the trumpet exceeding
> loud; so that all the people that *was* in the camp trembled.
>
> (*Exodus* xix:16)

IN THE MIDDLE OF the night, we are awakened by the racket of thunder made outsize and terrible here in this resonant echoing valley. A violent wind shakes our fragile canvas houses and threatens to blow us away. And our camels moan in the sudden and torrential downpour . . .

Wind more than rain is the enemy of the nomads. You have to get up and drive the stakes deeper, while the tents swell up, rip loose, and tear—and then you wait, trying to face up to losing your shelter in the frigid deluge: this is the impotent distress of the infinitely small faced with massive sovereign forces . . .

As the forbidding valley explodes outside with almost continual light, there is a terror of apocalypse. The valley seems shaken to its core, giving off muffled and crackling noise. You could say it is shuddering, opening up, caving in . . .

And then the bolts are slower and farther away. It all becomes something deep and cavernous, as if one could hear worlds turn in far-off voids . . .

And at last all is peaceful and calm . . .

Little by little we regain our silence, safety, and sleep.

❖ ❖ ❖

IN THE COOL, quiet morning at sunrise, when I open my tent, the outside air carries a whiff of perfume, so strong that it seems as if someone has broken a vial of aromatics in front of my door. And all this forlorn valley of granite is also perfumed, as if it were an oriental temple. Its few little pale plants, held back by drought, have awakened because of the night's deluge and waft their odors like countless incense burners. You could say that the air is ripe with benjamin, citronella, geranium, and myrrh . . .

Right off I look at the deserted valley, so strange and superb under the morning sun that is striking the red peaks into flame, against a backdrop of black, tattered clouds, fleeing fast to the north. The storm is still up there, while down here the air is slack and still.

Then I look at the ground, the source of all these perfumes; it is covered with white spots, like hailstones after a storm . . .

EIGHT

❖ ❖ ❖

And when the dew that lay was gone up, behold, upon the face of the wilderness there lay a small round thing, as small as the hoar frost on the ground.

(*Exodus* XVI:14)

W HAT WAS SHREDDED and left by wind and rain around our tents last night appears to be manna . . . I pick up some of these "small round things," these very hard white seeds, smelling something like cheese—they are the dried fruit of the thorny little plants that carpet these mountains here and there.

By collecting this manna, I have stirred up the perfumes of the soil, and for some time my hands give off an exquisite scent.

NINE

❖ ❖ ❖

ALL MORNING LONG through endless monotonous valleys flanked with red granite, we climb by imperceptible degrees toward the great Sinai, where we will arrive tomorrow. Valleys widen and mountains rise. Everything becomes larger under shifting dark clouds. Through enormous stone gaps ahead of us, we can now see even higher peaks, covered with white snow, sparkling against the gloom of distance and sky.

And an icy headwind comes up from the foothills of the Sinai. We are soaked with driving rain, sleet, and hail. Our camels cry out and shiver with cold. Our light clothing of white wool, our thin Arabian slippers, everything is quickly drenched with torrents of water—and we ourselves are shaking as if mortally wounded, with our teeth clenched and our frozen hands in pain.

During a calm we pitch the noon tent in a sheltered spot, a kind of granite hollow, hemmed in and made ominous by dark clouds. Our Bedouin start a fire of aromatic little branches, which smoke and flame mightily, and we sit down around it, everybody huddled close in the shared need to get warm and not to suffer any more. With their naked black arms and legs, their furry rags, their unkempt heads, their monkey-squatting, the others seem to be prehistoric animals around a primitive fire.

When we get up to set off again, some big green scorpions, also wanting to get warm, come up close to us and the multicolored rugs we are sitting on. Our Bedouin throw the creatures into the hot cinders of our fire, where they writhe and burn.

❖ ❖ ❖

DURING THE AFTERNOON we see all around us a change in the color and nature of stones. The granite becomes more crumbly and bland. Under the cold weight and half-night of a winter sky, we go through several valleys of flat sand, bordered by small clumps of camel-beige rocks. No more of those sharp angles, those jutting peaks, or those recent fractures we had around us for two days. On the contrary, we now have masses of smooth boulders that seem malleable, and strange formations take on the shapes of animals. You can imagine masses of monsters, pachyderms, salamanders, larvae, or clumps of dismembered arms and elephant trunks jumbled and joined together. At the barren intersection of these rows, imagined elephant or sphinx heads, perched like lords over this pile of shapes, seem to absorb and *sustain* the region's desolation. Millennia of isolation, sun, and rain were needed to sculpt and polish these disturbing creations. And silence yet. Still no one. Chanced upon some little birds of the same neutral color as the stones, and a few lizards as scaly as crocodiles. The sky is funereal and heavy, deepening the bleak enormity of the place, and from time to time snowflakes or hail fall on us again.

❖ ❖ ❖

IN THE WINTER TWILIGHT at around a thousand meters of altitude we make camp, surrounded by nightmarish rocks. We are now at the entrance to a broad valley, a kind of plain, seemingly walled in all around by a mass of dead monsters.

Among those huge fossil beasts that surround us, our Bedouin seek shelter and light fires under paws, under heads, under bellies, polished almost to a shine. The leaden sky blends with earthly things in dark confusion. But a glint of bright daylight still persists, allowing us to see into the depths of this enclosed plain, just far enough so that we can sense how forbidding those depths really are.

And snow is still falling, falling on our lonely camp.

Then we realize that we are not really *men of the tent*, in spite of how attractive a nomad's life might seem on beautiful sunlit days.

The *man of stone houses*, who was created inside of us by ancestral teaching, is vaguely uncomfortable having no roof, no walls, and knowing that there aren't any anywhere in this dark wilderness of appalling size . . .

TEN

❖ ❖ ❖   *Thursday, March 1*

And mount Sinai was altogether on a smoke, because the
Lord descended upon it in fire: and the smoke thereof
ascended as the smoke of a furnace, and the whole mount
quaked greatly.

(*Exodus* xix:18)

I N THE MORNING WHEN we break camp, the sky is brighter and the
snow has stopped. But huge clouds stand motionless against
giant granite cliffs, which are everywhere, rising up on all sides
above masses of petrified beasts and whose presence we had not
suspected in the murky darkness of yesterday.

We set off again on our climbing path through fearsome
gorges, like sandy corridors, lined with battlements ever higher,
higher, and darker. We leave the area of gray animal shapes and
enter the fierce and precipitous brown granite formations. The cold
worsens, and the air is getting strangely resonant. At noon, during
our rest time, when our Bedouin pass (a chilled lot in this icy
gloom), their racket echoes and reverberates like the fugue of great
organs in vast cathedrals. Far off there are tight black expanses, and
in their center the dead white of snow bursts forth here and there
through mysterious streaks of clouds settling in.

Hour after hour everything becomes more gigantic. And finally toward evening, among granite peaks shrouded with clouds,
the high ramparts and the few cypresses of the Sinai Convent can
be glimpsed, through white flakes that streak the air. Alas! How
silent, sinister, and cold this most holy mountain seems, whose very
name was still burning in us before we arrived. No doubt the time

is long past and forever lost when the Eternal One came down in
clouds of fire and terrifying trumpet calls. All of that is over, and
the mountain now is empty, like heaven and our modern souls; it
carries only vain, icy pretense, which the sons of man will soon have
stopped believing . . .

Our tents are already pitched among old crumbling abutments,
in a gorge where the wind blows wild and where the white shroud
on the land is strewn with our things. Our lonely camp is in sorry
disarray, caused by these blasts that threaten to blow it away and
this snow that is now a blizzard. Shivering with cold in our soaked
burnouses, we dismount from our big beasts; they are suffering and
complaining, nervous about this white curtain of snow, this driving
wind, these mountains so high . . .

Truly the night layover here seems impossible to manage, so by
messenger I send the Father Superior of the Convent a personal letter of recommendation, which the Patriarch at Cairo was nice
enough to provide. At the same time, I let him know of our distress,
asking him to grant us a campsite against the walls as shelter from
the icy blasts.

❖ ❖ ❖

THE ANSWER IS SOON brought to us by a young Father in black robes
who speaks a bit of French: "There isn't," he said, "any decent
campground near the convent. In our gorge there isn't enough
space for a tent between the rocks and the ramparts. But, if you so
wish, you could sleep in the convent itself and stay as long as you
like."

We accept the offer, begging the monk to stay and share our
evening meal before entering the convent. And we sit at dinner together with a freezing wind outside, while our Bedouin constantly
brush off the snow collecting in dangerous amounts on our tents.

But here comes the harried brother-porter, clutching a big
lantern and enormous keys: "Never," he says in Greek, "never never

has the door of the convent stayed open so late! By most special grace they have waited for us until now, but we must come in right away, or else be left out in the storm all night."

So, leaving everything behind, we hasten to go Indian file by lantern light. You have to hold on to your billowing burnous with two hands, and in spite of sinking ankle deep in the white drifts, you climb, climb in the murky night past granite boulders and rockslides.

For fifteen or twenty minutes we climb, with our feet bare, our slippers lost, sliding at every step in the snow.

At last we come to a wall that seems gigantic and whose top disappears in the dark, and a little very low door opens, entirely covered with metal at least a thousand years old.—We go through.—There are two more little doors like that one, servicing a vaulted passageway as it winds through a rampart. The doors shut behind us, with a metallic clang.—We are in.

And the whole thing, our clothing included, vividly recalls the Middle Ages: a nocturnal appearance of Saracens in a castle of olden times . . .

We are still climbing, this time on steps of rough-cut granite, and we go up a series of ramshackle stairs, deeper into this fortress, where strange clusters of little Arab dwellings wobble and melt together in our flickering lantern lights. We are to stay on the top level, in a kind of hostel for pilgrims, where the simple and primitive rooms all open onto the same long balcony and its rickety railings.

Hospitable monks, wearing black robes and hair as long as a woman's, hasten to comfort us with a little hot coffee and with glowing coals in copper vessels. Easygoing poverty and Eastern dilapidation seem to reign in this convent some fifteen centuries old. Our rooms, all alike, have the appearance of the poorest Turkish dwellings: whitewashed walls, ceilings and windows of unpainted wood dirtied by time, wide couches covered with the faded flowers of old calico throws. And in each of our rooms on a bare wall, a modest icon framed in white wood, lit by a burning lamp.

On our extremely hard couches, which must have been used by a multitude of pilgrims, we spread out sheets and coverlets as stiff as cardboard, and there we lie, glad to have shelter, hearing the wind and snow raging outside, thinking of our tents left behind, of our poor Bedouin, and of our poor camels we couldn't possibly bring along, and who are lying out there with no shelter under a shroud of snow.

As I fall asleep, I read inscriptions riddling the chalky walls: names of pilgrims who have come here from every corner of the world, Russian names, Greek names, Arab names—and a single French name: "Prince of Beauvau, 1866."

Little by little the wind subsides—and a total silence spreads through the night over this "haven of retreat" . . .

ELEVEN

❖ ❖ ❖

THE LITTLE NIGHT-LIGHT has been sputtering in front of the icon and finally goes out—at the same time as I am being awakened by bells ringing matins, with silver echoes in the supreme silence.

Then I drift off again, until the moment when I see a jet of bright sunlight filtering through the wooden slats of my window.

Opening your door gives you a shock of surprise, almost of amazement, at the strangeness of the place . . . In the cold light of morning, the fantastic things that we only glimpsed last night when we arrived are now present and very real, oddly arranged, as if pasted onto each other in two dimensions. And they are now astonishingly sharp and clear, because the air is so pure—and they are mute, mute as if they had died from their thousand years of old age. A Byzantine church, a mosque, little dwellings, cloisters; a tangle of staircases, galleries, and arches, descending to the cliffs below; all done in miniature, jammed into a tiny space; all surrounded by fearsome ramparts thirty feet high, and all clinging to the sides of the mighty Sinai. The long, lopsided, twisted, and decrepit porch our cells open upon is itself a part of this ageless group of constructions. Some of these are almost in ruins, having taken on the red coloration of the original granite; others are chalk-white, with painted accents in every conceivable Eastern color on their worm-eaten wood. You realize just by breathing the very crisp air that you are at a very high altitude, but you are surrounded by higher things, as if you were at the bottom of a well. All the highest peaks of the Sinai rise up, jutting into the sky, like titanic walls, jagged and grooved, made completely of red granite—but blood-red, without flaws and without shade—too steep and going too high, enough to almost inspire dizziness or terror.

The patch of sky you see is of an extremely intense blue, and the sunlight is magnificent.

Sparkling snow still powders everything in sight. It crowns the top of all the old walls with white velvet. Here and there the snow's white line betrays grooves in all the tremendous granite formations—which you can trace all the way to the dazzling top by arching your neck.

And the same unearthly silence permanently encases this fairyland monastery, whose great age is enhanced by its sun and snow. You feel that this is indeed the "haven of retreat," surrounded by wilderness on all sides.

❖ ❖ ❖

ON OUR PEACEFUL AND sun-drenched veranda, we stroll dressed like Aladdin, because in deference to the monks, we had our most attractive Asian silk robes brought from the camp. We even think that our outfits, each of which vies with the others, must look very good against the backdrop of old white chalk and red granite rocks. But nobody is here to see us . . .

From time to time, a monk with white hair and black clothing goes at an old man's pace up or down little staircases in this labyrinth, then enters some vault and disappears quietly into a cell somewhere. And immediately the deathly quiet returns . . .

However, the likable Father Daniel, who supped with us in our tent yesterday, finally appears and suggests that we go down with him to the church, situated down below our pilgrim quarters. We follow him through a series of little corridors, stairs, and vaulted passageways, where melting snow is dripping. Everything is twisted, warped, and worn. There are old doors of Arabian or Coptic style, the former sculptured, the latter inlaid. There are Arabian, Greek, and Syrian inscriptions, the youngest being centuries old . . .

Finally, at the end of the hollow that we had entered, is the basilica. They open wide for us the cedar door, which was carved thirteen hundred years ago—and we enter the astounding glory of this place, a place unique in the world, that has been protected by its location in the wasteland from revolutions, from pillage, from all human intervention, and that has remained about the same as when Emperor Justinian had it built in 550 A.D.

Your eyes at first are dazzled and disconcerted by the profusion of lights, silver lamps hanging overhead and forming above the mosaics on the floor a kind of second vault, suspended, complicated, sparkling.

And then you are struck by the almost barbarous antiquity of this sanctuary, rather than being struck by its wealth. It is a relic of times gone by, amazingly preserved. You feel you are transported to a primitive and magnificent past—so near and yet so far that it disturbs the spirit.

The heavy columns have irregular and semibarbarous capitals. The walls are covered with Byzantine paintings and gildings, marble mosaics, old faded embroideries, and old pale brocades. The whole back of the church is in almost Arabian Byzantine style, artlessly overdone, and, according to Greek rite, the tabernacle is hidden by a veil made from one of those wonderful Persian cloths that sultans used to wear long ago.

Through a little, very low side door behind the veil, we enter a most surprising place, where the tabernacle is kept. Here the vault is of gold mosaic, as at Saint Sophia, but intact, a priceless relic that the surrounding desert has preserved. The tabernacle and bishops' chairs are of delicate marble inlay; the cloths of almost unknown style have matchless faded embroidery. There are two reliquaries made completely of embossed and engraved silver, given by Russia for Saint Catherine. On both reliquaries the Saint is dressed in gold encrusted with turquoise, rubies, and emeralds, and lies with her head on a silver pillow whose exquisite and wonderful carvings imitate the texture of ancient painted tents.—Now you come to understand why powerful walls are necessary to protect such treasures.— All around are silver, gold, and jeweled icons hung on marble partitions. And on stands are gospels, parchment manuscripts a thousand or twelve hundred years old, bound in precious stones and gold . . .

TWELVE

❖ ❖ ❖

And he said, Draw not nigh hither: put off thy shoes from off thy feet, for the place whereon thou standest is holy ground.

(*Exodus* III:5)

B EHIND THE TABERNACLE is the most sacred place, the crypt of the "burning bush," where one of the monks leads us in cavernous darkness through even lower little doors. In a kind of vestibule, where the old oriental rugs are as thick as velvet, he stops us and has us remove our shoes before entering: in accord with the commandment of *Exodus*, you must enter this holy sanctuary with feet bare. At last, after crossing the threshold, we are transported to the sixth century and its primitive marvels of times gone by.

The dark shadows here are entirely decorated with vivid blue antique tiles and gold mosaics, all outshone by gold icons and precious stones encrusting the walls. The whole setting is lighted by a mass of silver and gold lamps hanging from the low ceiling. Rigid saints watch us come in. They are dressed in silvery robes, and their faces are barely visible in the shadows cast by their barbarous sparkling crowns. We must have anticipated their attention, or else why did we get so dressed up! Truly we would have felt like profaners of the past splendid and primitive artists, painters, enamelers, and goldsmiths, if we had come here in the clothes of our wicked and impious century. Never, anywhere, had we had such an impression of going back into the distant past. Generations, peoples, and empires have flowed by like rivers, while these precious little things have been here, safe in the same spot, shining with very slightly tarnished brilliance. Even this monk who is guiding us, with his long reddish hair covering his shoulders and his pale ascetic good looks, must be in every way similar to the illuminati of ancient times, and his understanding of things must be infinitely different from ours. Even this soft ray of sunlight, coming through one tiny window and drawing a kind of ghostly circle over the icons and tiling, seems to be ancient light, light a thousand years old . . .

In the back of the crypt, where lamps are lit, is a kind of chamber, veneered with elaborately cast silver. It is there that, according to venerable tradition, the *angel of the Eternal One* appeared to Moses in the fire of the burning bush.

THIRTEEN

❖ ❖ ❖

THROUGH THE USUAL little stairs and low vaults, we get to other chapels; narrow, obscure, mysterious, they are cut here and there into niches of the time-worn maze, among the sordid cells and wretched shelters. They all contain astonishing ancient things, which will soon be turned to ashes by the years, worms, and mold.

There are libraries also, each no larger than a ship's cabin, containing only unique and irreplaceable objects. One is filled with Syrian manuscripts. Another has Greek Byzantine documents from the same period, old priceless parchments illuminated in the silence of palaces and cloisters, books written by the very hand of Saint Basil or Saint Chrysostom, gospels in the beautiful script of Emperor Theodosius . . . Dust has been eating into them for centuries; and the winter snows melting on the roofs have sweated through rotting ceilings and splattered the treasures with black spots, as is still happening today.

❖ ❖ ❖

AFTER LEAVING THE glacial humidity of the cloisters and chapels, we make our way around the ramparts along the surrounding paths, on the high, chalk-white terraces where the Arabian sun flames and heats, in contrast with the snow nearby and the piercing wind.

From that height you can see down the red granite cliffs. At the cold, shaded foot of the cliffs are huddled a hundred-some Bedouin in dirty rags, hungry people arriving from the far reaches of the desert. Soon there will be the distribution of bread, an event that takes place three times a week. Never do the monks ever allow a single Bedouin to enter the narrow doors of the convent, no doubt for fear that he will take note of their riches. But two brothers of a lower order are stationed in one of the lookouts that project over the cliffs. In ancient times, when the gates were never opened, the lookouts were where the monks hoisted pilgrims up in baskets.

When the hour of alms arrives, the brothers drop a rope from a pulley. The Bedouin run up, each attaching a piece of their clothing to the rope. Then the rope goes up loaded with an enormous bunch of rags. Then a monk pulls out one of the rags and waves it above his head, shouting:

"Whose burnous is this?"

"Mine," comes a voice from below.

"How many are there in your family?"

"Seven!"

Seven black breads are wrapped in the burnous and from a height of thirty feet the bundle is thrown off the cliff . . . And so on, until the last.

To these poor people in the shadows below, we must seem like princes of *The Thousand and One Nights*, sporting our silk clothes in the sunlight above. But these great protective walls won't separate us from them for long. Already our tents and possessions, still out there, are inviting their curiosity—and we ourselves will be subject to their mercy, when we again take up our nomadic life in a less traveled and less secure direction.

❖ ❖ ❖

RIGHT NOW WE HAVE to decide once and for all about how to go through the Petraean desert.

So we have long talks with our guide, with the Arabs of our escort, and with the informed monks of the convent—a Tower of Babel conducted in Greek, Arabic, Turkish, French, and English. There is the added complication of the interdiction against Bedouin in the monastery; thus ours, sitting in a circle on the granite down below, are having their separate discussions in the chaos of red rocks; and every time we must ask their opinion or tell them some-

thing, we have to rush down on a series of crumbling little stairs
and go through the triple doors of the ramparts.

Finally we reach our decision: our most trustworthy Bedouin
will leave tonight on our fastest camel, to seek out the rebel sheik.
Our messenger will take him the letter from the Seïd Omar, another from the holy *hajji* of Mecca, recommending us to his good
graces, and a third that I myself wrote, asking him to let us pass,
also asking what kind of ransom he would require of us and how
many days he would keep us with his tribe.

Our trusty Bedouin is also to inform the sheik that we desire a
written answer, signed by him and waxed with his seal; and that we
shall wait for his reply here within the convent walls; and that if his
answer is negative, we will go back to Suez, renouncing the Arabian desert in favor of going to Jerusalem by sea. But these state-
ments are pure ruse and lies, for we will leave the convent in three
days to get ahead of our messenger (whose trip is to take six days
and seven nights) and wait for him at a certain spot, three stops
from here, where two valleys cross, one of which leads to Petra and
the other to Nakhl. If the answer is negative, or if the messenger
doesn't return, we will head toward the Nakhl Oasis, going around
the great sheik's territory, with his being none the wiser.

❖ ❖ ❖

NOW FOR THREE DAYS more we are the guests of this gloomy convent
that we were planning to leave tomorrow morning. Now that our
decision is made, we feel a melancholy sense of pause and peace in
this "haven of retreat," where we will be for so many hours more.

Seeking the last rays of sunlight, we walk along the highest
ramparts. It is scarcely four o'clock, and already the sun is disappearing behind the fearsome granite peaks that crowd the sky, like
monstrous screens jutting above our heads with such harsh, aggressive, and startling clarity.

The sun winks out, masked suddenly by one of these dizzying

peaks of rock, and immediately a very cold shadow falls on us, while the peak opposite will remain bright for a long time yet, glowing as seen from the half-dark where we are. And the peak is an almost hellish red against the raw blue of the sky.

❖ ❖ ❖

FATHER DANIEL, WHO HAS finished his religious duties, comes and asks us to go down with him into the gardens. Once again we descend deeper into the monastery's bowl, this time to go outside its walls. The air gets colder and colder; you have to bundle up and hang on to your billowing burnous with both hands.

The gardens, created with steady effort against the mountain's aridity, are in successive terraces surrounded by great unfortified walls; obviously, in case of siege they would be abandoned. There are cypresses, olive trees, grape vines, and a few lemon trees with leaves reddened by snow and hail. Under mature trees in a kind of forsaken enclosure called *mortification* by the monk in his bizarre French, there is the community cemetery, where the unknown and unnamed sleep the sleep of supreme renunciation. Here we are immersed in deep twilight, whereas over our heads the threatening overhang of granite is still awash with sun. It gets so cold we have to go back in.

Before leaving the great ramparts, we stop to inspect the first of the little low doors. Overhead are stone lookouts for throwing boiling oil and water on any besiegers. Above the door are two marble plaques, one in Greek, the other in Syrian, stating that this convent was built in the year 550 under the reign of *Justinianus, imperator*.

It is time to hurry back in, because the three iron doors are to be locked for the night. As we climb the little sets of steps and ramps, the Father describes sieges suffered by the convent, with Saracen armies sweeping down from the north and east, and the Bedouin dug in at these walls and threatening to plunder the holy treasures . . . Bewitched by these tales, we feel like men of the Middle Ages. Then we climb as high as we can, and from our vantage point on the terraces above the ramparts, we watch our messenger disappearing into the desert in long camel strides . . .

Then night comes, with a deafening silence.

And we return to our bare little rooms, where the glow of the icon lamps wobbles in gentle icy gusts of air.

FOURTEEN

❖ ❖ ❖ *Saturday, March 3*

A FREEZING WIND AGAIN, sweeping the sky ablaze with light. However, we can see snow melting slowly in the folds of the towering red granite.

There is a killing cold in our stark little rooms, where the wind slices through all the cracks of old wood. So we prefer to use up our time of retreat outside, strolling on the little terraces or under the little vaults, in the little stairs or along the very old little galleries that lead to the tiny chapels of antiquity. The silence is incredible. We are located in ruins, in the home of the dead. And since this necropolis lies at two thousand meters of altitude, lost in lands stripped of any human or animal life, the air here is pristine, almost virginal.

At long intervals we have the comings and goings of a few silent monks. Some of them slip by overhead and some below, all hastening to burrow, using doors like catholes in nooks of reddish clay. These are old men with long hair, looking like troglodytes coming home to caves.

The cats are like us. Roaming silently on the little sheltered roofs and on top of the little walls, they seek a bit of this warm sun that will soon disappear behind the awesome mass of granite above.

What loneliness here, and what sepulchral peace, with the feeling that you have nothing but the shroud of endless wilderness on all sides!

❖ ❖ ❖

AT CERTAIN TIMES of the day or night: Whump! Whump! Whump! In the bell tower a monk is using a large mallet to strike in a special way and in a strange rhythm on a long suspended piece of wood—a vestige of some tree from the time of the Greek emperors. It is the wooden clapper, an ancient instrument used in the earliest churches, when the Saracen tyranny forbade the clang of bells. The wood gives off dry thumps, hollow as the sound of bones clunking together. Now slow and now fast, now separate, now two in quick succession—all according to fixed rules over a thousand years old, the notes seem a mysterious secret language.

Summoned by the clapper, the monks come out of their little oratories and their little cells, from up above, from down below, from all of their barren holes in the crumbling clay walls. Around twenty of them, for the most part old and bent, with long white hair and long white beards hanging over black robes. They head toward the basilica staircase, going past the astounding cedar doors and slowly entering the incomparable sanctuary.

❖ ❖ ❖

IN THE EVENING, like captives in ancient citadels, we stand on a projecting ledge of the high ramparts, the only place where you can glimpse the distant wilderness of sand through a gap in the surrounding cliffs.

And we can see large black clouds coming from the depths of that threatening horizon. A groaning wind pushes them toward us. They climb very fast, darkening the sky and laden with more nighttime snow.

It is sundown, and the doors of the fortress are being locked below, under our feet, separating us from the cold desolation all around.

Then the monks come to inform us, while wishing us goodnight, that a caravan will leave tomorrow morning after the liturgy for the small port of Toba and will deliver our letters to the outside world, should we so wish.

FIFTEEN

❖❖❖ *Sunday, March 4*

W E ARE ALREADY used to "the haven of retreat" and its maze of little buildings, which are everywhere, apparently deliberately jumbled together.

We now understand this place better. All in all it is a square, seventy to eighty meters on each side, a kind of deep bowl with ramparts to defy assaults and the centuries. And in the center, this marvelous lead-plated granite shrine that is the basilica.

Between the ramparts and the church, there is a pile of random little constructions made of clay, wood, and plaster: a kind of oriental village, stacked up in a tiny space and inhabited by silent old men, who are the guardians of thousand-year-old relics. From time to time, near the durable church, the little earthen houses cave in and are rebuilt as before, without changes, using the same primitive procedures. Their only claim to individuality is their crude antiquity, however, with exquisite little details here and there: an old door of Coptic design, carved in cedar and ivory; an old window fretted with Saracen scalloping; an old delicately chiseled Arab work in marble.

❖ ❖ ❖

LAST NIGHT THERE WERE strong howling winds and snowstorms. But it all stopped before dawn.

And this morning the clapper and the Sunday bells sound through the calm air, calling the monks to the basilica. When we open our doors onto our overhanging veranda, the Arabian sun, very radiant, very hot, is there to distract and dazzle us. Roosters crow in the walled garden, and a dog barks. There is a kind of life-music vibrating and reverberating in echoes from wall to wall of the soaring granite. And a springtime charm, welcome and strange in this home for phantoms, floats in the warm atmosphere. It is almost hot, despite the snow remaining in shaded spots.

❖ ❖ ❖

AFTER MASS FATHER DANIEL comes to see us. His French, learned from a book in two months, is still childish; he always conjugates his verbs quickly, in a whisper, before using them. Showing me a fresh panther skin drying in the sun: "That one, your Grace . . . " Then he rapidly conjugates under his breath: "I eat, you eat, he *eaten*, we eat, etc.," and he continues, very sure of himself: "That, your Grace, he *eaten* camel. Yes, yes, that one little, he *eaten* camel!" Panthers are numerous, so they tell us, along the desert path we have chosen.

❖ ❖ ❖

THE BASILICA, WHICH THE monks have just left, is filled this morning with the Sunday incense, which is still floating as a light gray mist, half-way up the columns. We come upon the brother with the handsome waxy face and long curly hair who opened the holy crypt for us the other day, and who is one of the rare young men in the community.

With traditional deliberation, he is concentrating on lighting the silver night-lights. Set in this background of gold aged by the centuries, his pallor and his enlightened gaze almost inspire a religious fear, so much does he resemble a living Byzantine picture of the Christ . . . Oh! The strange ascetic face, radiant and grave, in the magnificent halo of reddish hair! . . . Now in this haven of dreams, the resemblance slowly becomes more real, and one could say he's no longer a living icon but the Christ Himself, the Christ concentrating humbly on human needs in surroundings so old that they seem like His place and His time . . .

He is, however, just a simple brother, dedicated to the small menial tasks of the church and to the maintenance of fires. He is the one who patiently shows us the sanctuary in detail, and by removing the brocaded dust sheets, he exposes marble, mosaics, and gold and silver icons.

Then, as requested by Father Daniel, the brother opens for us the tabernacle's two great silver reliquaries, which were sent some time ago by a Russian emperor. They contain church ornaments, cloth from the twelfth and thirteenth centuries, and vases and crosses of ancient design.

But from a third reliquary of plain marble, he takes two very large chests carved in gold. They contain relics that are more poignant. In one is the mummified black hand of Saint Catherine, lying with its rings and bracelets on a silk cushion. In the other chest is her head, crowned with a tiara of precious stones, an awesome relic framed by quilting and smelling of mummy . . . Then the chests are carefully closed, for years at a time no doubt. The heavy marble lid of the reliquary is drawn again over the two gold chests, and the dust cover of exquisite pink brocade is spread on top.

While the monk leans over to smooth the wrinkles in the cloth around this kind of coffin, the curls of his hair fall against the magnificent silk, and you think you see a shrouding Christ . . .

❖ ❖ ❖

BEFORE SETTING OFF into the wilderness, we would like to see the burning-bush crypt again—and we enter one last time, barefooted, trailing our white robes on the carpet.

Nothing has changed here since yesterday, indeed for a thousand years. The tiny window, deep as a fortress lookout slit, sheds the same light as before through its ancient stained glass on the glaze and jewelry of the walls . . . The saints and martyrs still have the same stare, encircled by their halos of precious stones and gold. And, so it seems to us, this monk with the long red hair and the handsome innocent face has totally become the Christ—the Christ in a simple black robe surrounded by these riches all around, actually living and moving near us. His presence here is no longer very surprising in this ancient setting, a setting that resurrects holy ghosts . . .

❖　❖　❖

ANOTHER PLACE OF ghosts and dust is a dingy room adjoining the Greek parchment library. Here the gospels written by Emperor Theodosius are preserved. A research room for monks and visitors. Through semicircular arches, it is dimly lit in the Moorish style by an inner courtyard. An admirable Persian marble fountain seems out of place there, and the seats, which are treated as ordinary everyday pieces of furniture, are armchairs from the Middle Ages in the form of the letter X that should be in a museum. Ancient portraits of saints and bishops hang on the walls, and through other arches one can see tiny gloomy oratories, where lamps are burning; these are nooks of mystery and death, stuffed with strange relics of antiquity. The overall impression is one of deterioration and irreparable decay. Everything is small, constricted, and stifled, due to the limited space within these ponderous ramparts—and the melting snow leaks from the ceilings drop by drop, like the sweating of caves.

❖　❖　❖

HOWEVER, OUTSIDE THE sun is beating down warmer than ever. There is a real Sunday silence and peace floating today over the reverberant convent, while the old roofs slowly lose their white shroud left by recent nights. The snows are melting. All the cats have come out looking for dry, sunny spots; and there is a monk walking surrounded by cats—he is around a hundred years old and is excused from the rules, very stooped, with long white hair and muttering a steady stream of rosaries.

In the lonely garden at the foot of the great ramparts down

below, there seems to be spring in the east; gray olive trees, almond trees all white with flowers, and deep-pink pear trees stand out in fresh and bright tones on these relentless backdrops of red, jutting, grooved granite rock, which take the place of the sky here—a sky so high above that it can be forgotten. And this spring is unique, seemingly come only to this incongruous garden and this cemetery laden with trees, since nowhere else would a garden find any place to grow in this huge expanse of sand and dead stones . . .

❖ ❖ ❖

THIS IS OUR LAST day here. At sunset we climb as usual to the highest terraces where we can see a bit of horizon through a slit in the enormous mountain rock. This time we study the little patch of desert where we will be tomorrow. The sky out there is calm, quiet, clear, and no new storm is foreseeable for our departure.

❖ ❖ ❖

IN OUR PART OF the convent, our presence has raised a bit of life. The ascetic monks, who could offer us bed but not board, have allowed us to bring in our Syrian servants with our provisions.

At least this evening our people have real kitchens, and they are fixing a lamb bought from the Bedouin down below, because Father Daniel and Father Econome are to share our last supper—a farewell that will be forever . . .

SIXTEEN

❖ ❖ ❖ *Monday, March 5*

THE SUN IS UP and the monks, weary from night duties, are still asleep when we go down the monastery stairs, and we pass, for the last time in our life no doubt, through the triple metal portals that date from Justinianus, imperator.

Not a breath of wind. Snow still lying above our heads. And nothing but a thin layer of white frost on the ground and things nearby. The weather is bright and wonderfully cold.

Continuing down for a quarter-hour on rock slides littered with enormous pink and red boulders, we finally get to our camp, where there is a frantic racket. Our tents, our baggage, all our things are in disarray on the sand. Camels are everywhere, and there are around fifty Bedouin in a bunch, all yelling at the same time.

The problem is that today our trip into a different territory means we have to change sheiks and escorts. So there is the inevitable heated discussion between those we are leaving and those we are taking on.

Also, the new sheik, instead of sending us the twenty camels we had requested, has sent us thirty-five; he wants to stick us with them so that we would have to pay a larger sum. But this negotiation is the problem of our interpreter-guide. To maintain propriety in the desert we must take no part in the discussions and must show a detached dignity by just sitting and waiting.

We are in a kind of mountain crater, where a glorious morning sunlight is beginning to shine. All around and pressing near us, the gigantic bluffs of pure red climb a sky of pure blue.

The bottom of this gorge has a very different sand, made of pink granite dust, dotted with blue pebbles, and dusted with white frost. Naturally, and forever, the green touch of trees and grass is missing here. But placed on this powdery soil of such a rare hue, our scattered things seem to be trunks painted every color of the rainbow in variegated arabesques. Along with blankets and rugs, with their dazzling splashes of color. And especially the huge camel sacks, decorated with designs of white shells and pendants of black wool—considered a great luxury by the nomads.

In the midst of these things, a constant frantic gesturing by the Bedouin. They are people with skinny bronze faces, waving long naked arms that poke out from ragged burnouses. And against the dirty black of their rags and pelts, there is the shine of their long copper pipes, their old copper rifles that have killed a lot, and their old copper cutlasses that have sliced into a lot of flesh . . .

And the dry granite is so resonant, it seems that people are howling above our heads at different heights from gorge to gorge of red rock climbing toward the empty sky.

At times the racket is violent and the gestures fierce. Here and there pairs of men clutch each other's heads in a kind of solemn oath.

Everything seems to calm down. And then they start to have the camels kneel so they can be loaded, and we see that we are about to move on. But a new subject for debate comes up, and we lose all hope of leaving.

Sometimes two or three suddenly quiet men go off alone to recover away from the group. After smoking their long pipes they come back refreshed and start yelling all over again.

Father Daniel and Father Econome come down from the monastery to wish us a final farewell. They support us by getting involved in the discussion and seem to be heard with respect, especially in their role as dependable bread-givers to the hungriest tribes.

Thanks in part to their intervention, the whole ruckus is finally over, after five hours of screaming. Everything is settled, and we shall have only twenty camels.—We mount and set off.

❖ ❖ ❖

FOR HOURS WE GO into either silent or resonant valleys of geological oddities, sometimes hemmed in by brown or pink granite outcroppings, sometimes in the crumbly grayish granite, worked and polished by rain since the world was and looking like heaps of animals from before the flood.

This time we are not in separate caravans and will not have our provisions precede us, because of the arguments this morning. And we have the additional company of the fifteen or so camels and drivers we refused, and who are on their way back to their tribe. Without the slightest malice, they are escorting us, chatting and singing all the while.

Little by little we descend from the Sinai heights, slowly regaining the welcome heat down below. And toward evening we arrive at desert sand, just the same and as expansive as ever, with its little light green plants that are perfumed and aromatic.

❖ ❖ ❖

AT SUNSET WE CAMP among these scanty plants of precious scent, with infinite emptiness all around instead of the cold weight we felt when the red granite boxed us in for four days. And Mount Sinai, now far away, has been restored to its dominant size in relation to the surrounding mountains. It alone tosses a snowy head above them.

It feels good to wear thinner veils of white wool in air suddenly warmer and saturated with odors, with horizons far away, swept clean for some time of all the crushing chaos of rocks. And we go on, feeling liberated and safe around our tents, while we study in the twilight the rougher, scrawnier, darker Bedouin who make up our new caravan.

At the arrival of the starry night, the sand keeps its warm and reddish tint, of an exquisite delicacy that we had forgotten and on which the camels and shrubs are scattered dark spots. Our Bedouin sit around their fire; the bright flames and the white aromatic smoke leap up toward the blue-black sky, where the zodiacal light floats. Constellations shimmer and seem either very close to the earth or magnified by huge mirrors. Then in the seated groups, a musette begins to moan, and a ragged, almost silent chorus joins in. Timeless music of the same kind made by the earliest shepherds, music that trembles, hesitant and fragile, in a staggering silence . . .

SEVENTEEN

❖ ❖ ❖ *Tuesday, March 6*

WE COME OUT OF our tents into cold morning splendor. A fine dust of white frost covers the sand and the pale aromatic plants, the myrrh, the absinthe, and the hyssop.

The plain has taken on its neutral, daytime color. But beyond the flat circle of the horizon all the granite teeth of the Sinai range rise up as if from pits below. They are deep pink, a radiant pink like that of translucent stained glass leaded in iris blue. Compared with the colorless and dismal desolation where we are, one could say we are seeing a fairyland that is not part of this world and that is separate and ephemeral in the empty sky.

Ice crystals sparkle on the canvas of all our tents. In northern countries you would suffer cruelly from such cold if you wore our light clothing with chests bare; but in this blaze of light and sun, the improbable frost is scarcely felt. And the air is so dry, so bracing that our clothes are doubly effective for survival.

There is a lot of noise around us at sunrise this morning. All the Bedouin dismissed yesterday and who slept near us last night say they cannot go on without some sort of payment and demand of our new men some of what we gave them. So the noisy arguments are on again, again delaying our journey. But today it is with an almost laughable lack of sincerity—it is just a need to yell, to expand the chest, to fill it with enough pure air for shouting, exactly like animals, like our camels, which every day roar at the rising sun like wild beasts . . . And the virginal light of seven o'clock glorifies these men in filthy rags, ennobling their clothes and broad gestures as if they were gods . . .

❖ ❖ ❖

ON AND ON FOR hours in the plains, under the burning sun and the icy wind, constantly crushing pale perfumed plants.

As monotonous as the sea, the desert also has its sea changes. Day before yesterday we had giant granite rocks; yesterday, flat sand; and today we enter an area of millstones, and their novel variety provides many surprises. We have just come upon a baleful maze of valleys composed of those yellowish and white stones; their horizontally stratified walls give the impression of man-made constructions having regular layers. You think you are going through destroyed cities, walking on streets, the streets of giants, among ruins of palaces and citadels. The structures rise in successive layers higher and higher, more and more superhuman, taking on the forms of temples, pyramids, colonnades, and great isolated towers. And death is everywhere, sovereign death, with its silent threat . . .

From time to time our drivers sing—a sort of sad lament extending through descending modulations to finish in a dirge. As usual in this world of brittle stones, their voices rouse vibrations and sustained echoes in this resonant void.

The most abundant plants here are almost colorless and fill the air with perfume. They smell like pippin apples in the heat of the sun, but with more of a bite and peppery odor. Gazelles apparently come from afar to graze on them, because we see imprints of very delicate hooves in the sand; and the prints are widely spaced, consistent with leaping beasts, searing the sand with rapid flight . . . And suddenly some gazelles appear, scampering like the wind on the crest of fantastic ramparts! They quickly disappear from view into the blinding white, far away . . .

❖ ❖ ❖

AFTER THE NOON STOP, when we have slept on the heavily perfumed sand, our heads wrapped in our white burnouses, our waking gives us a kind of desert anxiety that we had scarcely felt before.

And this anxiety gets worse during the afternoon, while our camels continue to sway us along in these same threatening valleys, which seem like intimidating ruins, both huge and wild. Our feeling is indefinable, a wish for *somewhere else* no doubt, a regret for the springtime we are losing now, a spring that in other countries would bring green things and flowers. Here, nothing, ever; it is a cursed part of the earth, which is willfully isolated and where man should not come . . . And, at the mercy of our Bedouin guides, we go deeper into this land, on and on, on and on, into a great unknown that gets darker and darker despite the burning sun, and which seems to breed unimaginable mute threats of harm . . .

❖ ❖ ❖

BUT EVENING COMES, evening with its magic, and we let ourselves be charmed all over again.

Above our tight little camp, around our harsh horizon where the threats seem momentarily appeased, the twilight sky ignites a matchless border of pink, orange, and green, which climbs slowly to the peaceful zenith and goes out.

It is the delicate and charming moment in the dying light that is no longer day but not yet night, when our perfumed fires begin to burn bright, sending their white smoke toward the stars. This is the moment when our camels, relieved of their loads and saddles, brush through little bushes and graze on perfumed branches like outsized, fantastic sheep moving at a slow and passive pace. It is the moment when our Bedouin sit in a circle to tell stories and sing; the moment of rest and dreams, the delightful moment of a nomad's life . . .

EIGHTEEN

❖❖❖ *Wednesday, March 7*

T HE SUN IS GRADUALLY hotter and the wind gradually warmer as
we move away from the high plateaux of the Sinai desert and
descend toward the Gulf of Aqaba.

All morning long we continue as before, among titanic ruins of
ramparts, temples, and palaces . . . For thousands and thousands of
years, weather, rain, and landslides must have worked here with incredible slowness, laying the hardest seams bare, destroying the
softer veins, digging, sculpting, crumbling, with the guile of art and
symmetry, to create this frightening and superhuman impression of
an endless city, which we have been in for twenty leagues.

Toward noon the desert becomes rather black, everywhere as
far as the eye can see. Rather black also its sand, littered with black
pebbles. Even the palest plants have disappeared. It is absolute desolation, the great uncontested triumph of death. And above it all
lies a heavy, mournful sun, which seems destined only to kill by de-
hydration! . . . We have not yet seen anything so threatening. We
choke in searing darkness, where any light from above seems to
bleed and die. We are in a kind of devastated world, depopulated
by fire, that will never again be nourished by moisture . . . Gradually the vague anxiety of yesterday grows into anguish and fright.

❖ ❖ ❖

BUT TOWARD EVENING we arrive at "The Valley of the Spring"
(Oued-el-Aïn), where we will camp. It is the first oasis since we left
Mount Sinai, and it seems an enchanted place to us, as it suddenly
unfolds like a new theatrical set, between two high mountains. The
oasis is enclosed and wonderfully protected by rocks that have suddenly appeared, similar to those of Mount Sinai, but even deeper

red in color. In the distant center of it all there rises a kind of temple, a kind of Hindu pagoda, a bizarre geological quirk, an enormous perfect pyramid, flanked almost symmetrically by bell towers and turrets. Its base is of a color so intense that you could say it had been rubbed with blood, while the peak, made of a different granite no doubt, lightens and turns sulfur yellow.

Against the dark red of all those great rocks stand groups of palms so green as to appear almost blue. Some of these palms are in thick clumps on the ground, while others rise up on long leaning stems. And tamarinds and reeds, with flowing water rushing over stones! Our parched camels bellow on their way to fresh water and wildly dunk their overheated heads. And after our days of depressing visions, we are drunk with the splendor of this hidden Eden, and we happily set up camp in its triple amphitheater of bleeding rocks and beautiful blue-greens.

Here we are to meet the messenger we sent to Mohammed-Jahl, chieftain of the Petraean desert. Our man should have been here before we arrived. We will wait for him one day, then two, but if he doesn't return, we'll have to take the alternate route toward the Nakhl oasis. However, our Bedouin don't seem very worried about heading toward the great bandit without authorization.

NINETEEN

❖ ❖ ❖   *Thursday, March 8*

O H! THE OUED-EL-AÏN, the Valley of the Spring! What words could one use, what fresh phrases could one borrow from the poets of the ancient East, to paint this Eden hidden in desert rocks?

It is morning, brilliant morning, and I wander through the delightful oasis where our little village of white canvas is to remain for one or two more days. At the bottom of the valley, there is a swift and bright stream in beds of pink granite that have the shine of polished marble and that have no plants or algae; the bottom is clearly visible, like that of the artificial pools built for the baths of sultans and houris. The rare water, the precious water flows, sometimes hidden in distant pink turns of the streambed, sometimes overflowing along its path into small sandy bogs, where reeds, tamarinds, and superb palms are spread out in all shades of blue.

You are struck with admiration for each of these primitive groves as you walk by. Then this little paradise is suddenly hidden behind enormous granite rocks, and all you can see for a while are the polished stones of the stream—until the moment when the miracle revives at a turn and another enchanted grove appears. The sky is by nature crystal pure, as a sky in Eden should be. And birds are singing in the palms. Dragonflies tremble on the rushes. In spite of the overhanging rocks, sparkling sunlight races and dances on the ribbon of the moving stream.

❖ ❖ ❖

IN A DEEP BASIN with gently sloping sides and which seems like a king's sumptuous sarcophagus, I stop walking to take a swim. Then, looking up, I catch sight of huge prehistoric beasts, leaning over the the cliffs above and looking at me with their necks stretched out as if they knew me: it's our camels! No doubt they are pondering how they can get down to the treasured water, and they must also be appreciating this pleasant morning in their own way.

You can go everywhere in the oasis barefoot or in light slippers. The rocks have been worn so long by the patient centuries that now they are shiny and smooth, with no sharp edges. Otherwise there is sand as fine as velvet, where you see human tracks mixed with the tracks of panthers and gazelles. And in this part of the world, where rain, smoke, dust, and sweat are unknown, you never get your clothes dirty; you can walk anywhere or stretch out on the clean dry ground without soiling the long veils of white wool you wear—and under these veils the sunlight and invigorating breezes harden and tan your chest.

❖ ❖ ❖

THERE IS A SPECIAL peace, a matchless peace in this unspoiled oasis, surrounded and protected on all sides by the dead immense desert. So we spend our waiting hours here in no special hurry.

A single moment of excitement today: there was a very large snake discovered in a palm tree. Our Bedouin saw it, but we didn't, and they say that it had two heads and thus was *Barkil*, king of snakes, and that it must be killed. So by throwing stones, they made a futile racket among the beautiful groves of palms.

TWENTY

❖ ❖ ❖ *Friday, March 9*

Yesterday evening we had decided not to wait any longer for our messenger, who was probably lost, and to leave today for the challenge of Petra anyway.

But this morning before daylight, I hear very loud handclapping behind the canvas of my tent, near my head. This is the way they wake up our caravan. And the relieved voice of our interpreter-guide yells to me in Turkish: "*Bizum adem gueldi!*" . . . (Our man has returned!) He has brought a very good letter from the great sheik!" . . .

I reply: "Come in, come into my tent, and show me the welcome letter right away."

Preceded by the long ceremonial lantern, he enters holding an envelope stamped with the seal of Mohammed-Jahl.

After the Arab greetings, we find that the Sheik of Petra wishes us safe journey, and states that he will meet us in Aqaba with an escort and camels. He also promises to have us in his territory for a total of twelve days while helping us on to Palestine. His letter ends like this:

"In the name of Allah, who is all, and not in the name of the sultan of Istanbul, who is nothing!" MOHAMMED-JAHL

❖ ❖ ❖

We break camp with more enthusiasm than usual, but with regret for this place that none of us will ever see again and that is especially charming in the morning sun.

While we are bathing in the pink pools, and while they are saddling our kneeling camels, we see last night's dramas etched everywhere in new tracks on the sand—pointed hooves of gazelles and

claws of panthers. The Valley of the Spring is a daytime oasis of silence; and it becomes at night a gathering place for beasts that keep
a watchful eye on each other. They come from far and wide to
drink at this stream, a stream like no other . . .

❖ ❖ ❖

WE LEAVE THROUGH the far end of this special place, negotiating difficult trails around the red mountain that looks like a Hindu
pagoda. For an hour or two we are in chaos, a chaos from some recent cataclysm: living landslides, mountains still crumbling, valleys
that are just beginning to form. Projecting out over our heads, piles
of stones threaten imminent disaster. Whatever remains up there
seems so off-balance and frozen in rockslides caused by such
minute and random forces, that it seems possible to remove just one
tiny pebble and unleash terrifying rockslide after rockslide, each
one dragging another along. Such permanence and such silence
give you the strange feeling of visualizing the forces that must have
shaken the desert very recently and swept it with storm after storm.

But we have already come across other dying areas like this one
today. This is how all of Arabia is being dismembered and destroyed bit by bit, its having no real dirt or plants. It seems just a
withering pile of bones. At times its mountains collapse; then the
centuries pulverize them, turning them slowly into sand that is
blown down toward the Red Sea by winter winds and rain.

We decide to continue on foot behind our camels past these
jagged mountains with their sharp ridges. It is obvious that at any
moment a vibration, or the tone of a human voice, could set off an
avalanche. Likewise our single-file steps and the swaying of our
camels could unleash a storm of stones . . .

❖ ❖ ❖

AS WE LEAVE THIS menacing region, we are happy to regain the
desert and its monotonous calm.

When the great desert changes color, it almost always does so all at once. The mountains, the ground, and the plants change together into the same new color.

So from now until evening, we have the kingdom of gray, a flat gray, as if powdered with ashes and veined here and there with burnt sienna.

These are the foothills of the Djebel-Tih mountain range that we will cross tomorrow, through its gloomy passes with steeper and steeper walls. At the dark entrances there are tight little valleys, whose desolation is stifling. There are other, larger ones, whose greater desolation inspires an almost sweet resignation to the great eternal sleep and the end of it all . . .

Gray are the high peaks, gray the stones, gray the leafless little plants. And a wind has come up, swirling this heavy omnipresent sand like ashes—while clouds of the same gray as the earth race across the sky in a mad flight to the west.

During the noon stop in a rock hollow, where our laid-out rugs seem even brighter compared with the grays all around, two cooing wagtail birds, who had been following us, come over with clever boldness and eat our bread crumbs. No doubt the few living beings here have a kind of pact and a truce on killing . . .

Ever higher these mountains and cloudier the sky. At some turns in the gorges the wind howls furiously.

To my surprise, collected some violet flowers, similar to bear's-ears, which grow occasionally here and there.

During a rainstorm toward evening, in the darkest of the valleys, hemmed in by the ever higher ash-gray mountains, we come across a nomad family. The half-naked man (he is armed to the teeth) and his woman have three children. The youngest, three to four years old, is adorable and charming, with his long black hair blowing in the wind and sitting astride his veiled mother's shoulders. Their camels also have a baby that is gamboling wild. Their goats have several kids, which trot along bleating. Quite an itinerant contract, beasts and people helping each other, trying to multiply, to create life, despite the bad will of this land of death. They come from far away perhaps and really don't know where to find anything better. The father, after greeting us timidly with the polite phrases, could see that we had no aggressive intentions in spite of our number, and he asked the vital question: "Have you found water?" We reply, "Yes, in the Valley of the Spring at so many hours to the west." Then we lose sight of them at a bend in the gray labyrinth.

Ashes, more ashes. We seem incapable of escaping the flat grays with their crumbled and powdery look.

We camp in a little featureless plain, where it becomes dark while the sky is still light because the plain is walled in, boxed in on all sides by steep mountains thousands of meters high, which seem to be nothing but gigantic piles of ashes. The narrow path by which we came here and the one we shall take to go out tomorrow are two deep, black fissures opening gloomily onto dark areas. We are at the base of the highest foothills in the Djebel-Tih, and we must cross them to descend into another desert . . .

There are a few small trees, still without leaves, the melancholy spring of this place being slow to grow in mountain shade. Thorny and dwarf mimosas like the ones we came across some time ago.— And no water.

However, close to us there is a camp of two or three Bedouin families with black tents. In contrast to our accustomed isolation, they assume the dimensions of civilization. Some goats and kids that have grazed on vegetation somewhere are led back to their woolly fold by little girls.

This hour of pastoral calm is strange in such a place, and you tremble as if experiencing the most primitive human eras when you hear the nearby wailing of a shepherd's musette.

❖ ❖ ❖

AFTER AN EXCHANGE of messages, both we and our neighbors feel more at ease. A little girl even dares to come into my tent to offer some of her goat's milk. She is quite pretty in her childish apprehension, and she opens her wonder-struck eyes wide: this tent is lighted with candles and embroidered from top to bottom in very bright colors. Perhaps it goes beyond whatever her young primitive imagination had ever been able to conceive of earthly splendor.

❖ ❖ ❖

NOW IT IS NIGHT. Above the high ash-gray wall that cuts off half the sky, a thin crescent appears like the white of a fingernail. This is the first moon of Ramadan, in the land of Islam an almost sacred moon that marks tonight as the beginning of the month of fasting and prayers.

TWENTY-ONE

❖❖❖ *Saturday, March 10*

W HEN OUR GUIDE CLAPS his hands to wake up the camp, it still seems to be night. The truth is that we are in the dark shadow of the overhanging mountain. But the sun has risen behind this curtain of ashes, and its rays are already bursting onto the hazy distant peaks.

We start the five-hour trip through the Djebel-Tih gorges.

Gone, yesterday's ashes. Now we have pink granite rocks, whole worlds of pink, seeming like huge slabs of marble streaked here and there with blue. We keep going in dark and churchly silence, following natural corridors that are like cathedral naves enlarged beyond any human scale, to the point where you feel dizzy and afraid. In these trails, which must have opened during the first convulsions of the earth, countless centuries have created a luxurious soil by fragmenting the peaks, then leveling everything that fell and pulverizing it so fine, so fine, to make a sand that is more pink and bright than what is found on beaches. You could say these are smooth and rigid rivers of sand, where all the pillars and all the battlements supporting the huge walls sink and die.—We who are so small and who are preoccupied with smaller and smaller things, we must have such places as this land that neither man nor verdant nature has ever touched, so that we can understand a little better what the formation of worlds and the magnificent shocks of those births must have been like.

Not a single plant around us. We are in a very pink land, marbled with light blue. Even the shadows, the somewhat tunnel-like shadows created by all the granite above us, have taken on a pinkish hue.

There are some straight passageways and others curved with sharp turns. Sometimes the nave we are following seems to end, but it bends into the mountain and continues in another similar nave. A deathly silence of nature, with a resonance that magnifies enormously the least brushing of a burnous or the least murmur of a voice.

❖ ❖ ❖

AT A TURN IN one of these corridors, we encounter a nomad tribe on the move. Coming out of the dim light ahead, one group after another appears as if materializing from the rocks. Our camels flare their nostrils and complain as the strangers go by.

The men are the first to appear; they are heavily armed, dressed in rags, and look mean. They greet us right off with the brotherly gestures: they touch themselves three times, on the chest, the lips, the top of the head, and then in pairs they lean their foreheads together with a kind of kiss in the air while shaking hands. When the greeting is over, the newcomers break into broad, toothy smiles, suddenly childlike and sweet—and move on, reassured and friendly.

The female camels appear then. They are accompanied by their little ones, which have the innocent expression of sheep and which jump up and away when they see us coming. The mother camels bear the old men, all with white beards and white hair, all wearing blank tribal stares.

Then, with light and silent step, the women appear, mysterious in their black, ghostly veils. As they pass they raise their shining eyes, which flash black lightning at us from the slightly raised folds of their veils . . . Among them there are nursing-age children and puppies riding in baskets on donkeys.

Finally, along with herd dogs, the older children bring up the rear, adorably fragile and expressive little boys and little girls, driving the frightened flock of bleating goats and kids.

Black, the clothing worn by the women; black, the cloaks of the men; black, like polished ebony, all the goats with long, dangling ears. In the cool of the morning, in the half-daylight of these deep gorges, and against a pink background and pink mist, it is a long, black procession—the large beasts at a loping pace, the men at a dignified and easy pace, the herds in ragged formation, with stubborn stops that bunch them into an impeding mass of wool . . . As long as this parade lasts, the usual silence is replaced with the dull thud of steps in sand and with muffled voices under veils. At times, from deep in their throats, the camels add their raw grunts, which rebound like little thunderclaps along these resonant walls.

❖ ❖ ❖

WHEN THE TRIBE HAS gone by and disappeared, we find water, a real stream that is flowing and meandering over the sand. Unfortunately this water is loaded with naphtha, sparkling on the surface in oily blotches; but it has sustained life anyway: there is grass on the banks, and there are tamarinds and high palms like those of the Oued-el-Aïn, so green that they appear blue. The whole scene is hidden perfectly in the tumult of pink granite rocks. A touch of Eden for half an hour with background music coming from the song of resident little birds.

But at another bend in the stone corridors, the stream disappears and with it the magic green things. We are back again in dry, silent, dead desolation. And the sun begins to appear in the narrow ribbon of open sky between the great peaks; it stabs us with burning rays.—No doubt the cool water and blue palms we have just seen were merely a dream . . .

❖ ❖ ❖

FINALLY, ABOUT ONE O'CLOCK, through a wider opening (apparently the last) in the Djebel-Tih range—a horizontal band begins to appear, still far off but of a special color that we had almost forgotten in our world of pink—a band of wonderful lapis blue: it is the Gulf of Aqaba, and we have made it to the other side of the Sinai peninsula!

The opening widens. The bluffs are less numerous as they move away from us and sink into the distance. We finally arrive at the shore of this sea, which is a blue intensified by the salt desert of its beaches.

Contrary to the Gulf of Suez, used by all the boats in the world, this Gulf of Aqaba never sees smoke or sail. A route abandoned for a thousand years, it is at present a lost sea, pushing in vain against impenetrable deserts. Above its water on the other shore shines something unreal and marvelous: the coast of Great Arabia. It is something that seems so near and yet so far, due to the sharp clarity of its summits: one could say it is a high wall of pink coral delicately streaked with blue, standing against the sky to lock the entire Orient off from the rest of the earth.

❖ ❖ ❖

CONTINUING FOR ANOTHER hour on the awesome sparkling beach, continuing along the infinite blue band, surmounted by the endless pink slash of desolate Arabian splendor.

And now an oasis is there before us, at the edge of the calm water, with bouquets of palms and blindingly white man-made constructions—they stun our eyes.

It is the little forward post of N'Nouébia, a citadel in a hamlet of dried-mud buildings, guarded by an Egyptian governor and a dozen soldiers.

❖ ❖ ❖

UPON APPROACHING THE OASIS, we are surprised to see our tents already pitched among the palms. We had requested that our Bedouin extend today's trip as much as possible, but it's only three o'clock, much too early for setting up camp . . . So here comes our caravan's sheik, with a look of disappointment: the *caimacam* (the governor) stopped him from going on and obliged him to camp here, where the official intended to detain us all until tomorrow morning!

"Where is this caimacam?"

"Over there in the citadel!"

The soldiers on guard (extraordinarily handsome Arabs in their long veils) state that he is resting. He is asleep because it has been Ramadan since yesterday, and the first fasting has worn him out . . .

They awaken him anyway, when I show how upset I am. And here he comes. He is a little, grotesque, and ugly person, wearing an attempt at a European suit. Among his handsome soldiers in robes, he looks like a monkey in a morning coat. He is one of those bureaucrats barely touched with a veneer of civilization who are so common, alas, in the East, and who make a bad reputation and create enmity for the noble races of the East. Already disagreeable in civilized countries, these small minds in the desert become petty kinglets who, instead of protecting caravans, stop and hijack them, causing them more harm than bandits or wild animals.

Standing outside in the scorching sand by the sizzling white-washed porch and surrounded by soldiers in burnouses, we all engage in a violent argument. He simply wants to dig into our purse. If he holds us back, it's to have the opportunity of forcing night sentinels on us and to make us pay a lot for them . . . Unfortunately he represents the authority of a large territory. He could have us pursued and could invent new problems for us in a world we don't know yet. So we have to appease him. I finally propose that we pay for the night sentinels plus a tip, if he lets us leave immediately. He accepts the deal.

❖ ❖ ❖

BUT THE DELAY HAS made us lose an hour. It is already rather late for folding up our tents and departing . . .

So, in good graces now, we shall be prisoners of this imbecile until tomorrow morning, and we will accept his superfluous guards.

To tell the truth, it's a delightful imprisonment, for N'Nouébia is an oasis of splendor and calm . . .

The Arab village, with its little houses of dried mud, is a bit farther on behind the citadel, but our little canvas town has been set on fine sand by the sea. The beach is strewn with red coral, large clam shells, large flesh-colored shells, and shells of pale peach-blossom pink.

It is evening. The motionless water of the gulf is green mother-of-pearl, with metallic highlights and reflections the color of exotic bird feathers. And standing above the water are the pink granite rocks of Arabia—but pink with a pink no words can describe—and these rocks climb high into a limpid greenish sky laced with small streaks of orange clouds.

None of any dazzling magnificence I had seen in my whole life on earth could compare with this . . .

❖ ❖ ❖

now the sun is hidden from sight behind the mountains of our shore. But Great Arabia over there can still be seen, for it glows like a signal flare; it is a jumble of live fires and pink coals, rising like a wall into the darkening sky, while the desolate sea at its feet seems to have become a light itself, perhaps an emerald plain set on fire from down below.

In front of this immense spectacle, which goes on as far as the eye can see, stand the palm trees, more delicate in silhouette, displaying their very fragile plumes.

Our watchmen arrive, serious and handsome, with their nearly divine faces under white veils and their braided cords of black wool. They are quiet because the hour of the holy Maghreb is here, and they sit in groups on the sand, around piles of branches that they will light for the night—and they wait . . .

Then all of a sudden, from the top of the little citadel dominating the town, the voice of the muezzin rises, a high-pitched and bright voice that has the somber and gentle bite of an oboe; it brings trembling and prayer as it soars through the air like the spreading of wings . . . Above the overwhelming magnificence of earth and sky, the voice sings, sings a hymn to the God of Islam who is also the God of the great deserts . . .

Then night comes with its transparent blue haze, where the distant granite of Arabia is slowly dimming its glow. Little wood fires leap up around us, lighting here and there the undersides of date palms, backlighting palms and the Arab guards sitting in circles under the great dome of a night all ablaze with points of gold . . .

At last the voice of the muezzin sings a second time, more beautifully and on a higher flight of prayer—until the moment when we will lose touch with reality, stretched out on the comforting sand under the brilliant light of the stars . . .

TWENTY-TWO

❖ ❖ ❖ *Sunday, March 11*

W E GET UP EARLY today for a long trip to make up our lost time. At dawn already our Bedouin are busy around us under the tall palms. By the fires that burned all night, our magnificent guards are standing in their white veils and black cloaks. The children of the village and a few veiled women are staring at us; no doubt the big event of our stay will remain engraved in their memories.

When our camels come to us and kneel, our guards approach to shake our hands and, like children, to wheedle exorbitant amounts of money from us. But they themselves are smiling at their unacceptable requests, which punctuate their wishes for safe travel as our great animals rise and carry us away.

❖ ❖ ❖

ON OUR WAY, along the seashore. And as soon as the charming little oasis has disappeared, the open desert swallows us up again.

Everything that flamed red last night has gone out and has become transformed. The coast of Great Arabia has receded, receded into unmeasurable distance. After having burned so much the night before, the coast rests now in an exquisite morning freshness, half hidden under a humid haze. Now it is colored only in pearl-gray or flaxen-gray—it is totally softened, blurred and translucent. Just the upper jagged outline of its summit can be seen somewhat clearly; and tufts of clouds persist up there like light quilt wadding; these tiny tufts of a dazzling golden white seem to have absorbed all the light of this early morning.

In contrast with these nebulous and gray things, the shore where we are traveling, between the great bluffs and the sea, begins to dazzle our eyes. And its beaches sparkle.

70

The air is intoxicating to breathe. It seems that your chest expands to take more in. You feel rejuvenated with the physical joy of being alive . . .

This sea is so calm and so pleasantly iridescent. And we go along it on a fine sand sown with red coral. It has no port or sail. Throughout its whole length, a dead sea in a dead land. But it is still a sea; in vain do you know it is empty forever, you still approach it instinctively as a wellspring of life; when you are near the sea, you no longer feel the dead and ominous desolation of the earthly wilderness . . .

❖ ❖ ❖

AS THE SUN RISES, the coast of Arabia becomes gradually clearer, escaping from its morning dusk; its subtle outlines come alive and heat up—gradually becoming the huge splendid fire that will be this evening's spectacle.

Now we are traveling on shells, the likes of which we have never seen. Kilometer after kilometer, we see large church-font scallop shells grouped or scattered by the tides; then we see enormous fountain shells, shells of a porcelain pink that resemble wide-open hands; then there are giant turritella scattered or stacked. And the beach, now a solid white mother-of-pearl, glistens magnificently in the sunlight. An incredible mass of mute and slow living things, which have been tossed up here after having worked for centuries to hide the lack of purpose in these shapes and colors . . .

I remember that in my childhood dreams, during a temporary stage when I was taken with natural history, I sometimes saw exotic beaches strewn with astounding shells. All I had to do was lean over to collect the most beautiful and rarest kinds . . . But this real profusion before me goes far beyond what my childhood mind could imagine.

In remembrance no doubt of those old dreams, or perhaps through childishness again, I have my camel kneel, and I get down to study these shells. In addition to the three kinds that I have already named and that cover the beaches, there are also cones, porcelains, murex rocks, harps, all extremely delicately painted and in the strangest shapes; most of them serve as a home for hermit crabs and run away on tiny tiny legs when you try to touch them. And here and there big chunks of coral make red spots on these multicolored and mother-of-pearl displays.

❖ ❖ ❖

TOWARD NOON THE DAZZLING splendor reaches its peak. The total perspective of visible things no longer resembles anything we know. You could think you were present at some huge silent spectacle of the earliest geological periods—on earth perhaps or in some other world . . . The overall effect is pink, but it is streaked down the middle with a long endless band that is almost black it is so blue, and that would require pure Prussian blue slightly streaked with emerald green for a painting.

This band is the sea, the strange Aqaba Sea. It slices the desert in half, cleanly, brutally. It creates two parts, two zones the color of hydrangea, of an exquisite pink in twilight clouds. Alongside these waters of too blatant coloring and with too sharp contours, the rest seems misty and vague by dint of reflection and glare. There everything shines with pearl, granite, and mica, and everything trembles with heat and mirage . . .

One of these zones is the coast opposite, the Great Desert Arabia, spread out in reddish granite rock, a fabulous wall a thousand meters high, which rises mightily up into the sky as it fades away into the diaphanous distance.

The other zone is the beach, where our camels plod, all of pink sand, coral, and pearly shells. And beyond the beach are the bluffs of this shore, in the same granite rock as those of the opposite shore and with the same touches of cloud and flower.

Oh! The strange and unique sea, this sea of Aqaba, never tainted by sails, eternally mute, eternally hot, breeding its world of coral and shells in its blatantly blue water, framed by the changeless pink of its deserted and almost terrifying shores, where man appears only expendable, nervous, rare, and in constant fear for his life . . .

❖ ❖ ❖

AT THE NOON HALT, we pitch our tents and spread our rugs on thousands of piled-up shells—enough to fill the windows of collectors to overflowing.

Then, after a deep sleep, we continue our travel in light that is gradually more gold, gradually more pink. In the morning we went five hours, and we will go four hours more in the late afternoon, but always surrounded by the same magnificence. As we proceed, the Sea of Aqaba gradually narrows, and Arabia on the other shore comes closer to us.

All afternoon a crazy wagtail bird obstinately follows me, right in the shadow of my camel, fluttering and cheeping to avoid the long russet legs. Its cry and the crunch of the caravan on shells seem like loud noises in the midst of this silent and splendid world.

❖ ❖ ❖

AT TWILIGHT WE make camp on a beach where our camels find skinny plants to graze on.

And when my tent has scarcely been pitched, the pleasantly aggressive wagtail appears at the door, as if asking permission to enter and eat and to be protected from the desert.

We are right by the sea, in a sheltered spot that the great bluffs of this shore dominate. And they have already set us into dark shadow. At the same time over there, beyond the waters that have become the color of a peacock's tail, that chaos of granite that is Arabia has not yet finished its evening magic: between a green sea and a green sky rise mountains, the bases of which are of a violet found in bishops' robes and whose peaks are of an orange-pink— but an unusual, indescribable pink that persists after the sun has gone down, as if there were fire burning inside, as if everything were going to be melted together soon, as if the great furnace of cosmic creation had reignited into cataclysms and destruction of worlds . . .

However, all around there is a calm, a silence, a peace blanketing man and things indicating that these splendid shocks are merely plays of light and mirages, merely appearances, nothing . . .

❖ ❖ ❖

HOW WILD THIS place seems at mysterious nightfall! How far our little nomad camp is from the real world!

Behind us the granite bluffs have become very black screens, weirdly and solidly cut, rising against a sky of stars—and the thin crescent of the Eastern moon, with its two points sticking out, is poised overhead like the fierce seal of Islam . . .

But Arabia has burned out. Beyond the water that is beginning to rustle in the night wind, Arabia is just a grayish band, and it suddenly seems farther away. Our camels, fearful of the darkness and predatory animals, have come close to kneel by our fires. Our Bedouin are black-and-white ghosts you can still make out in the dark; prone on the sand of this forsaken beach, they are piously saying their last prayer before sleep. And the wind, suddenly stronger, colder, and more bitter, begins to shake our tents . . .

TWENTY-THREE

❖ ❖ ❖ *Monday, March 12*

O UR CAMELS STILL project long shadows on the sand and mother-of-pearl. Great Arabia over there is still wrapped in its thin cotton wadding, as we set off in the delightfully cool hours of morning.

Yesterday we went fifty to sixty kilometers. Today, in order to reach Aqaba—the only city that serves these territories and where the holy caravans rest—we still have around sixty kilometers to cover, in undiminished splendor, on the same quiet beaches of the desert, on the same layers of shells, along the sea without sails, with only us alive on its shores.

Everything today is as yesterday. We breathe the same invigorating silky air. The color of the water is of the same intense blue. The sand is reddened with the same coral, sparkling with the same scattered mother-of-pearl. And Arabia goes through the same hues, from hour to hour warmer and more beautiful—until the final moment, when the night magic will be displayed, as it was yesterday, day before yesterday, since the beginning of time . . . This is the prodigal land of fire, where every day magic tricks of light are played for no one to see.

It seems that the atmosphere is infinitely tenuous, almost nonexistent, because you can see clearly so far. You misjudge distances, and you find all measurements impossible. On each coast of the sea, the two symmetrical walls of granite unfold. Slowly and in step with our caravan, the summits and capes of the two shores continue, as sharply drawn in the distance as they are nearby; and yet they maintain an almost ghostly appearance, because they are so bright behind the waves of light endlessly fomented by the slightest breaths of heat. The sea alone, the extraordinarily blue sea with its extraordinarily sharp edges, seems something real and tangible. But one could say the sea is suspended in a vacuum, in a kind of great pink haze—and this is the terrifying and hard granite chaos of the desert . . .

Toward three o'clock, on a small island not too far from shore, our astonished eyes, which have not been used to seeing human constructions, perceive the ruins of a citadel and its black battlements in the Saracen style. It seems this used to be a convent of solitary monks in the style of the Sinai Convent. But this retreat has been abandoned for a hundred years.

The sea narrows gradually as we come closer to its end, and the coast of Great Arabia gets gradually closer, its granite wall reaching as far into the sky as the one on our side.

We are very impatient to see this city of Aqaba, toward which we have been traveling for six days. In the remote past, it was Ezion-gaber, where the Queen of Sheba disembarked and where the fleets of Solomon set sail for far-off Ophir. Later it was Aelana of the Romans, still flourishing some two thousand years ago. Now it is not even a port. For centuries ships have forgotten where it is, and Islam has cast its great sleep over it. They say that now it is only a vast caravanport, where pilgrims for Mecca camp briefly and take on provisions. But according to stories of a few modern travelers, it is still the city of portals decorated with arabesques, the city of beautiful clothing, of red burnouses and magnificent sights to behold.

Finally on the other shore, there begins to appear a row of trees, palms no doubt—a long green streak, surprising in the setting of pink hues. It must be the isolated oasis where this city is built. We will pitch our tents there in two or three hours.

❖ ❖ ❖

THE JUNCTION OF two desolate and silent little valleys is a perfectly dreary spot for our caravan to cross—and I would like to try describing this nameless desert intersection. At the end of the beach, these two valleys of death come together. The sea, still having its same blatant Prussian blue color, persists as the only truly solid and real thing, surrounded by a vague reddish or pink land, as if pow-dered with ash and hazy because of reflections and light. But, sur-prisingly, trees are here, and they add an indescribable excess of gloom to this dismal sight. Two or three thin date palms and weird doom palms with multiple trunks wave long erratic branches; and each holds aloft a bouquet of yellowed fans. These are plants of an-tedeluvian appearance, motionless in the sun, against the ashlike and misty background of the pink granite rock . . . A solitary stork that was perched there asleep spreads its wings to follow us. And my wagtail from yesterday flutters in my shadow and is still keep-ing me company . . .

❖ ❖ ❖

ANOTHER HOUR ON these beaches, and finally we reach the end of the mighty gulf that we had been skirting for three days. The Prussian blue water describes a curve that bends against the sand in a kind of final great circle, which we go around to reach the other shore, where the Aqaba oasis waits for us.

But if the sea is ending, the two walls of mountains that lined it are not. They still parallel each other northward as far as the eye can see; except that they no longer enclose water, just sand—and the gulf of Aqaba becomes a kind of endless valley, displaying a few broom plants, a few doom palms, and a few high majestic date palms.

This valley is the Petraean desert. Our drivers already feel ner-vous about entering the great sheik's domain.

❖ ❖ ❖

NOW WE ARE APPROACHING Aqaba, which seems to be nothing more than a thicket of palms, as silent as the surrounding desert. Not a house can be seen, no people either there or on the beach, and not a single boat on the sea. But dried bones in all directions, with animal skulls and skeletons dotting the sand.

It is the time of evening, the time of gold. On the trunks of the clumps of palms and on the long leaning stems of those that grow alone, the gold is overwhelming. But there is already twilight dark in the distance and in the shadow of these forlorn and beautiful trees.

We go under the palms, and their magnificent vault covers us immediately with shade. Still no one around, nothing moving, not a sound. But old and crumbling low walls, made of dried mud mixed with pebbles, skulls, and vertebrae, create pathways that we wander along. And this is the great Aqaba! . . . However, here are a few human beings, Bedouin camped within the walls in dirty gray tents and watching us go by with their casual curiosity. Through gaps in the black tangle of palms, we can see the magnificence of the sky, and we can see the chaos of the flaming pink granite as if it were the gleam of some distant fairyland . . .

❖ ❖ ❖

FINALLY WE ARRIVE at a kind of central square, where there are a citadel, houses, and men. And our tents, which preceded us, are standing there, the object of curious or hostile eyes. Over the citadel floats (in our honor, no doubt) the red flag with the crescent. The squat houses are made of dried mud and have the primitive look of animal lairs. The small group that is studying us is composed of a few common Turkish soldiers and superb Arabs, with their black cloaks thrown over their white clothing, the veils held on foreheads by braided black or gold cords. When we dismount, the Turkish soldiers come to us with a nice friendly attitude. So I speak the language of Istanbul, and I shake their hands. I'm very happy to see them here and to feel I'm in friendly territory.

Then they bring me a man representing the Sheik of Petra. He had been waiting for us here since yesterday and must leave tonight so that he can inform the great highwayman of our arrival.

I tell him: "Beg the Sheik Mohammed-Jahl to come tomorrow

and to bring twenty men with twenty camels, which I will rent
from him in order to cross his territory . . . "

"Camels, camels!" says our interpreter, who still isn't too sure
of his French. "I don't know what camels he'll bring, I don't . . .
Perhaps he won't only have any robe on his face! . . . " Translation:
"Perhaps they will not even have bridles or little muzzling straps to
lead them by . . . "

And this skeptical pessimistic man adds that the caimacam,
that is, the Turkish governor of Aqaba, is counting on my presence
tomorrow morning in order to speak of grave matters, probably to
forbid me the Petra route.

❖ ❖ ❖

WITH OUR CAMP PITCHED, curiosity satisfied, and groups dispersed,
we are now alone under the last rays of twilight in absolute calm.

I'm a little anxious about tomorrow's interview, as I sit in front
of my tent and watch the nightfall ending the marvelous twilight.

Almost all at once, in all directions of the sky at the same time,
the stars appear. And the crescent, still very thin, is already lighting
our world. Beyond the primitive and dreary little houses made of
soil and mud, the huge pink-gray desert and all its rolling sand
dunes and rock mountains rise, rise surprisingly high into this pure
and shimmering sky. They seem a diaphanous and stunning vision
of emptiness, very exquisite, but almost beyond belief and without
perspective. Against this immense nothingness, streaked with the
ghostly shapes of clouds, slowly and silently a few ghosts go by,
draped in a lingering blatant white or pitch black—violent shocks
in the murky pastels of the scene: these are camel herdsmen coming
back late to the oasis and driving their animals into large pens enlarged by moonlight. And one could say they are ghostly too, like
the landscape whose vague color they are . . .

Closest to us in this square of Aqaba where our tents are, lie
masses of black forms, distinct despite the dark—they are what we

have brought into this remote oasis, beasts, people, and things. There are sleeping camels, each one with its head plunged up to the eyes into a muzzlebag, which seems to give it a tapir's nose; Bedouin hunkered down or stretched out, who are silently smoking and dreaming; harnesses, blankets, caravan packs, and sleeping bags . . .

And behind me the black curtain of the palms, with large bouquets of plumes, masking the deserted beach where the sea murmurs its song in a silence without end . . .

❖ ❖ ❖

THE BEACH ATTRACTS ME, so I go and get Leo in his tent for a walk with me on the beach.

At first we have to go through the shadows of the palms, along sandy paths beside the low walls of the yards. Introspective as at the threshold of a temple, we enter the dark grove. We are both very Arab and very white, in the light fullness of the wool veils that cords keep on our foreheads. We're even a little like ghosts, with our inaudible step of Turkish slippers on layers of sand. In this grove there is a special aroma, a warm air that smells of the sea, the desert, and the wild. Above our heads bouquets of stiff black plumes go by in the still air, and one after the other, as we pass they stand out against the bright shimmering sky and the golden crescent.

Here is the beach, still pink as if it were still day—and empty and deserted, needless to say! Along its shores unfolds the mysterious and magnificent grove, which throws a darker night on the beach. The little walls of earth mixed with bones follow the curve of the beaches and outline this great sanctuary of trees. But here and there a trunk, separated from the grove itself, leans out and projects its spreading plumes. A vague image of it is reflected upside down in the water. Everywhere the sea seems surrounded by bluish mountains and seems small as a lake. It is very diaphanous at this hour of night, this boatless sea, misty and ghostly in a gray blur; but in the moonlight it shines as a stream of dull spangles.

From the totality and the silence of the scene comes a dark magic. It is not the languid spell of tropical nights. It is something far more overwhelming and austere: it is the nameless gloom of the Moslem countries and the desert. The rigidity of Islam and the peace of death are spread everywhere . . . And there is a very unutterable magic in being here, mute and white as ghosts, in the beautiful Arabian moonlight, under black palms, next to a desolate sea that has no ports, no fishermen, no ships . . .

TWENTY-FOUR

❖ ❖ ❖ *Tuesday, March 13*

A BAD DAY.—In the morning I go to the caimacam, as I am worried about the rumors that have reached me about his intentions toward us.

The khamsin wind blows, scorching hot, whipping sand and grasshoppers along.

A kind of little street leads to the caimacam's house, lined with scraggly molehill houses made of beaten earth the same color as the soil. His house is of beaten earth like all the others. I am led into a room with a very low ceiling that has a strong desert smell: rough walls heavily plastered with chalk, palm-tree trunks for beams, dried palm fronds for roof.

Here comes the caimacam, a Turk with a gray beard, smiling, polite, distinguished, but having a stubborn look. In this isolated place he could play cat and mouse with us. He has three hundred Turkish soldiers under his control for getting his way; besides, we can't be in open denial of an Ottoman authority.

"Travel to Petra?" he says. "No, not possible any more. A year ago Egypt ceded this territory to Turkey. To go there you would need authorization from the pasha of Mecca, who is now in charge of this desert. Unfortunately we don't have this authorization. Moreover, it would be too dangerous for us, because the northern tribes are in revolt. There's fighting over by Kerak, and the government has just sent three thousand soldiers from Damascus."

I propose to him that we send a fast messenger by camel to Cairo, in order to request of His Eminence Mouktarpasha the favor of a special authorization for us, and we would wait here for the answer; it should take twelve to fifteen days.

He refuses this solution as too extreme. "Foreigners," he says, "cannot stay for any reason more than twenty-four hours in Aqaba."

His final decree: We will leave tomorrow for Suez, back where we came from, and we will follow the same route as before.

Obviously he fears for our lives and doesn't want to be involved. Also perhaps he has new secret orders to keep this route closed to certain subversive foreigners, and he is applying the same rules to us without knowing to what extent we are friends of Turkey.

We had predicted all the setbacks, all the difficulties implied by this journey through Petra at an unsettled time—all the difficulties except an official refusal from the sultan's government; and nobody in Cairo, not even the friendly pashas who had been concerned about our trip, had told us that Petra was now in the possession of Turkey.

Devastated I go back to my tent. And Mohammed-Jahl, who is to arrive tonight and whom we wouldn't have irritated for any reason and who will probably shake us down for it! . . .

The khamsin blows hotter. Our tents are full of sand and flies. And having heard of our disagreements with the caimacam, the people of Aqaba are beginning to consider us as suspect.

Our only recourse left is Mohammed-Jahl himself. We get the idea of placing ourselves entirely in his claws: pretending to return to Suez and telling him to come with his Bedouin to pick us up at two or three days' travel from now, in order to lead us into his part of the desert. But would he cooperate? And for how much? And afterward, having violated the Turkish territory against interdiction, we would not be able to expect any help from anyone. What would we do, supposing we chanced upon the three thousand soldiers from Kerak, who would probably bring us back as prisoners to this same caimacam of Aqaba? . . .

However, anything rather than go back pitifully to Suez! And this Sheik of Petra, whom we couldn't trust at first, is awaited today almost as a savior . . .

We are assured that he will make his appearance among us at the hour of Maghreb . . .

❖ ❖ ❖

DURING THE AFTERNOON, the caimacam comes to my tent for our meeting. In spite of the heat, he is dressed in a long caftan of green wool, trimmed with civet fur. Just as courteous as ever, he apologizes again for being obliged to administer such a new regulation, but he remains inflexible, only granting us one more day to stay here.

❖ ❖ ❖

WHEN THE HEAT AND sunlight dissipate, I go, dejected, toward the shore.

The shore is just like yesterday evening, exquisite and desolate, the beach of the desert.

An Eden light, a light of enchantment and fairyland, radiates everywhere on the gigantic amphitheater of pink granite, where we see the death of the lapis sea, the sea that is abandoned and empty forever. The curtain of magnificent green palms billows in the breath of the khamsin. The little walls of beaten earth, dotted with whitened bones, tibias and jaws, decay in the dry heat. On the sand there are antlers of coral and a scattering of rare shells. Naturally not a boat in sight, nor a human being. Prominent in this glorious splendor there is nothing but a putrid camel carcass, lying with its innards gone and showing its vertebrae, in a twisted pose with a frozen gesture of legs in the air . . . Constant silence, constant the peace of death, and constant the oppressiveness of the immense desert lands all around . . .

At the hour of Maghreb, the great sheik has not yet arrived. He will assuredly arrive during the night, they say, and we continue to await him with a nervous impatience.

❖ ❖ ❖

AFTER OUR NERVOUS DINNER, the caimacam sends for our permission to have a second interview. We consent in hopes that he will change his mind. He arrives preceded with a great flourish of ceremony, sits down, chats in Turkish about any old thing—always very friendly—and takes leave without having said a single word about the burning question.

❖ ❖ ❖

AT NINE O'CLOCK IN the evening, I return alone to the beach, using a small descending path littered with all our Bedouin and camels: poor men and poor beasts, whose faces are now quite familiar to us, and who will take off tomorrow morning, turning us over to the unknown caravan that Mohammed-Jahl is bringing! . . .

The sea is making its muffled evening rush. The slender crescent of the moon of Ramadan is shining among the stars. The retreating tide can no longer be seen, and the bay has recovered its appearance of a tight little lake in the deceptive veiled gray of the scene, which is transparent here and there.

Two Turkish soldiers are sitting there on a stone in the shadow of the curtain of palms.

We strike up a conversation. In Aqaba they feel as foreign as I do. They suggest that we three stroll on the sand in the hazy light of the moon along the superb black palms.

They are brothers from Smyrna. They have left two younger brothers back home. Their exile has been for nineteen months and is to last a total of two years. Once a year a Turkish ship comes here to relieve the garrison; so in five months the ship will come to repatriate them . . .

The stench of a cadaver suddenly . . . Oh! We were coming upon the dead camel, the sole inhabitant of this beach. We can barely make out its pose and legs in the air by the light of this very new moon.—We change direction. "He fell there not seven days ago," they tell me; "but already the dogs and jackals have practically eaten him up."

I promise the two brothers that I will come again tomorrow night to talk with them on the beach about *back home*. I return to my tent for bed without feeling sleepy, expecting at any moment the arrival of the sheik who will decide our fate.

TWENTY-FIVE

❖ ❖ ❖ *Wednesday, March 14*

A T AROUND THREE IN the morning, the Turkish citadel sends out
a trumpet signal, a gravelly, shuddering, drawn-out, strange
sound that leaps up into the cool quiet of the night . . . Oh! How the
trumpets of Istanbul come back to mind because of this! . . . I know
what it is, however. We are in Ramadan, and they are warning the
faithful that the hour of fasting and prayer is now.

Shortly afterward a small drum (or the knock-knock of dry
wood) begins to sound in the distance. Then it comes close to our
camp and goes around it . . . Oh! How primitive, how primitive
and portentous it sounds in the silence of the night here, with its
echoes sustained throughout the desert . . . Slowly the drum strikes
its blows, three by three—thump, thump, thump!—thump, thump,
thump!—and its very slowness imparts an indefinable shudder to
these unknown rhythms . . .

Mohammed-Jahl arriving, no doubt! It could only be him, with
such music. I step out of my tent and ask the guards:

"What's up?"

"Nothing," they reply. "It's just a Ramadan signal to start the
prayers, like the trumpets a little while ago . . . "

Thump, thump, thump! Thump, thump, thump! With this
whump of dead wood, the procession circles our tents twice; then it
continues in the black paths of the oasis, and soon its noise finally dies . . .

Another hour goes by. Then I clearly hear camels arriving,
camels they are getting to kneel by yelling "Sss, sss." Then people
dismount, approach, and exchange ceremonial bows with our
guards—while a voice fearfully pronounces the name Mohammed-
Jahl. This time it's him, and I expect him to open the door of my
tent any moment . . . But suddenly, overcome by sleep, I lose aware-
ness of anything human . . .

❖ ❖ ❖

I T WAS INDEED Mohammed-Jahl. But he had pushed consideration to the point of trying not to disturb me on his account. And when he was informed about our unexpected difficulties, he had taken advantage of the old custom of staying up all night during Ramadan, and at three in the morning he had gone to plead our cause with the caimacam—to no avail . . .

The interpreter-guide tells me these things and informs me that now (eight o'clock in the morning), the great sheik would like to be brought to my tent.

❖ ❖ ❖

ACCOMPANIED BY TWO young men, his son and nephew, he arrives with his hand extended and a smile on his lips. He accepts a chair and takes his seat with a lordly grace—and I send the news to my two traveling companions that I have the bogeyman of the desert in my tent.

A fine and superb old bandit's face. Gray beard and eyebrows. A cameo profile. Flashing eyes, which on the spur of the moment can be imperious and cruel or else disarmingly gentle. He is dressed in a red Brusa silk robe embroidered with yellow flames; its dangling sleeves almost touch the ground; over this a generous Bedouin shirt the color of sand and dust; and on top a lambskin sleeveless tunic. On his head a veil (*couffie*) of heavy Mecca silk, held in place by a crown of gold cords with black wool knots. Tiny feet, bare in leather sandals; tiny child's hands playing with the traditional stick shaped like a lotus leaf that serves as a camel whip.

Very winning, superbly dignified. From time to time a flash of authority or fury in his shifting unpredictable eyes that turn away when you look at them, but which stare and see right through you as soon as you're not looking at him.

He is just as I expected, perfectly formed by fifty or sixty years of high banditry. And next to him these two young men he has brought seem like innocuous, docile, and fearful children.

He bids me welcome, expresses his surprise at the obstinacy of the caimacam and his regret that he cannot receive me in Petra.

"But," I say, forcing things, "couldn't you pretend to take us toward Suez, and then two days travel from here . . . who would be the wiser . . . "

He cuts me off by grasping my hand. The frustration of a captive wild animal passes through his shifting eyes: "Ah!" he says; "in the past, yes . . . in the past I called the shots. But now the Turks are here, you see, and a year ago I swore my loyalty, and I gave this caimacam my word of obedience . . . "

I now understand that our last hope has dissolved.

It is useless to argue, because once your word has been given (which counts for so little in the advanced countries of the West), it is absolutely sacred among the desert bandits.

❖ ❖ ❖

HE PROPOSES THAT we go back to Egypt, not through the Sinai again, but following the route of pilgrims to Mecca (Nakhl and the Tih Desert), which would take only ten days; and that I use the escort that he had prepared for me and that will arrive from Petra this evening, at the hour of Maghreb.

"Dismiss," he says, "your men and camels; you will take mine, for they are better."

I accept with thanks. Besides, refusing would get me nowhere, since I am in his clutches now.

So it is agreed, and we have only minor questions to resolve. First the fee for personnel and animals. He shows himself to be quite reasonable about the price. Then the question of the toll for everyone: "In the past," he says, "when foreigners crossed Petra I got twelve pounds in gold per person. I am asking only six for you, because you have only skirted my territory." It is a flawless deal, so we part the best friends in the world, with very cordial handshakes.

❖ ❖ ❖

THUS IT IS NECESSARY to fire these poor Bedouin who had led us here. But they were expecting it when they knew that I was in the power of the Petraean Sheik. Their packing was done and their skins were filled with fresh water from the oasis. As soon as they are released, they come to give us the farewell hand-kissing, very much in a hurry to get away from local dangers.

They were overall good sturdy people, born in the slightly more hospitable Sinai desert. When we watch them disappearing over the sand, it seems that our last tie with the world has just been severed.

❖ ❖ ❖

WE ARE TO LEAVE for Egypt tomorrow morning, with the twenty men and twenty camels rented from old Jahl. The mere thought of reappearing in Cairo is especially irritating to us. What will our friends say, when they had thought we were on our way to adventure, only to see us return like scatterbrained hikers brought back in a dog-catcher's cart, only because we didn't have the proper papers?

In all honesty we cannot adjust to it. At the risk of everything, we will really try en route to corrupt the people from Petra into changing direction toward Palestine. But this would be a bad move, exposing ourselves to all kinds of ridiculous complications, because we have violated the interdiction of an official Turkish representative. So we really don't know what to do, shut in our tents which the searing khamsin is filling with sand and flies.

The whole day drags, difficult and frustrating. But the oasis, and especially the area closest to us, is being strangely populated:

armed prowlers coming closer and closer to our canvas walls, Bedouin with sharp features or blacks with flat faces, all the wanderers, the starving, all the looters of the neighboring deserts, drawn by our provisions and our gold, gather around us like flies diving on food. And large locusts come too, blown in by the southern wind . . .

❖ ❖ ❖

HOWEVER, DURING THE afternoon and thanks to old Jahl, new discussions arise between our camp and the thatch-roofed house where the arbiter of our fate resides. Through the narrow little street with the earthen walls messengers come and go, keeping some hope alive for us.

The caimacam is extremely sorry to have caused us so much trouble. But letting us go by way of Petra is probably not a consideration, because he is afraid of jeopardizing his responsibility to his government and ours. It would be a bit risky too at the present time (an opinion even seconded by Mohammed-Jahl), as he can be responsible for us only to the limits of his territory. He also speaks with a certain amount of apprehension about the battles waged yesterday near Kerak and Tafileh.

But perhaps the governor will let us go directly to Gaza, by going straight down the middle of the Tih desert, a trip of ten to twelve days in regions even more remote than those of Petra and the Dead Sea. All this on the condition that we be escorted by a Turkish officer and two soldiers from the Aqaba citadel. And of course we would pay for the camels, food, and other costs as they might occur. This last requirement proves especially that he doesn't trust us and that he still harbors a deep suspicion about our being spies, because we have insisted on crossing, without proper authorization, the forbidden region where Turkey has just started military operations. But we can't really blame him for this suspicion, because the Petraean desert has nothing intrinsic to justify our obvious determination to cross it.

Toward evening matters seem to be improving. The caimacam, sequestered because of Ramadan, has us informed that he is exhausted from fasting and prayers, and that he begs us to wait until after Maghreb. When he has eaten and drunk a little coffee, his head will be clearer for a decision about us. So we are less nervous now, and the road to Palestine through the desert finally seems to be opening up.

❖ ❖ ❖

AT SUNDOWN I GO with Leo to bathe in the deserted sea. The prowlers with cutlasses that our presence enticed to the oasis hover around our tents—and through the palm grove the pathways lined with their ancient little bone-studded walls are as deserted as usual. The beach is also dead, along the eternally blue sea, at the foot of eternally pink mountains.

We walk to the end of the oasis, where the superb date palms end and are replaced with thin groups of palms that are stunted, scattered, and isolated in the desert sand.

After our bath we are stretched out, drying off in the shade of a couple of palms, and faint padding behind us perks up our ears. About a hundred sheep are running toward us . . . The shepherds appear. There are two of them, two Turkish soldiers in uniform, armed to the teeth, a repeating rifle on their shoulders, and their belts loaded with revolvers and shells—these are smiling faces I recognize . . . Well! My friends from yesterday evening, the exiles from Smyrna, Hassan and Mustapha, the two brothers. It appears that a part of their duty is to take the sheep of the citadel grazing.

"Are your sheep so vicious that you must be heavily armed to protect yourselves?"

"Oh! Not for the sheep," they reply. "No, for the Bedouin! The country around here isn't safe. At just a half-hour from Aqaba they are starting to cut throats!" . . .

Then they gather up their flock with shepherd calls, to take them back to their pen. I promise that I will come to the beach again tonight, two hours after Maghreb, so that we can chat one more time . . .

❖ ❖ ❖

AT EIGHT O'CLOCK IT is dark, and a very ceremonial messenger comes to our tents from the little dirt pathway. The caimacam requests that the Sheik of Petra and I come to speak with him. We go to him full of hope.

The aged sheik is the first to go in and sit down. Then we gravely do likewise, in this room of dried mud dimly lit by a lantern in a niche. The caimacam, wrapped in a fur caftan despite the heat, seems very tired from fasting, but he extends his hand in welcome. A black man brings cigarettes on a tray and coffee in china cups. Then after the protocol compliments, silence reigns.

The door opens again, revealing a piece of sky with black palms and a star. Then several characters enter silently, with solemn dignity. They are old men with gray beards and fur caftans; their heads are dressed with Mecca veils; they have set and unreadable faces, which have at first glance the beauty of the prophets, but with sharply hooked noses and eagle-vulture eyes. Judging by the caimacam's welcome, they must be influential desert notables. Their business, however, will be handled after ours, because they are seated off to the side, almost out of the light, in a row along the wall, where they form a fierce tapestry while our fate is being decided under this old ceiling of fronds.

Finally the caimacam starts talking, with an elegant and pleasant voice. In a thousand digressions, he tells us it is possible for us to go directly to Palestine, but he still has hesitations and fears . . . Oh! The slow pace of things in the East! . . . The conversation is in Turkish, with our guide on his knees before the governor. The guide has an attitude both supplicant and sly, watching and pressing for the definitive *yes* that would permit us to continue our trip—and a half-hour later, the caimacam deigns to give it! So we are saved, for he has given his word on the same basis as any other Easterner.

Now we just have to write our names and his in French and Turkish, arranging a few questions about detail. We take our leave, delighted after these two very anxious days.

❖ ❖ ❖

OUTSIDE THE NIGHT is marvelous, and here it is eternal night, the etherial night. Along the dark pathway padded with sand and under the shadow of the palms, I go dragging my ghostly white veils to spend my last evening on the beach by the sea lit by the crescent moon.

My two friends, the shepherd soldiers, had been waiting for a long time, despairing of seeing me again. Surrounded by the deep silence, we launch into conversation about the Turkish homeland, Istanbul and Ismir. We pace back and forth at the edge of the glittering water, with a little detour every time we approach the dead camel . . .

A distant trumpet, solemn, slow, and very high-pitched, like the voices of the muezzins, calls them back. They must immediately return to the fortress. They take off, pointing out a path that leads into the shadows of the palms: "Go straight through there. It's the shortest way back to your tents."

Now I'm lost, alone in the dark. The grove is not huge, but it is cut up in all directions by pointless man-made barriers and incomprehensible things in ruins. Many times I proceed between these old low crumbling walls into dead ends going nowhere! It goes without saying that there is nobody around, but there are bones and animal skulls, very white in the vague moonlight softened by the palms . . .

It must be near midnight, very late for Aqaba.

Finally I end up in a cemetery. How I got here I don't know.

But the vault of great black plumes is no longer above me, and I can now see a bit farther to get oriented . . .

A true desert cemetery in encroaching and eternal sand. It is a subdued pink in the light of the moon. The soil and the rough little tombs in the form of camel saddles blend into the same pale salmon color. Nothing stands out or attracts your attention. It all has the vagueness of form that is special to the things in this country at nighttime. One could say it is seen through a veil of rose gauze . . .

An animal was there eating something awful in a hole. It runs away with a little yapping that scares you to death—a dog or jackal.

The heavy palm grove that I have just left recedes and spreads into a curtain, and I am now faced with the vast emptiness that has taken on its nightly appearance. Above the walls of this cemetery, which seem to have gentle shapes, the dunes appear gently drawn also. And higher up in the distance is the massive granite bulk of the mountains, extending to the lunar crescent a kind of rushing pink rising tide. It upsets your sense of perspective, as if the earth had become smoke and had floated over there to turn upside down. But this fragile balance endures, and everything remains fixed, frozen forever in eternal silence and calm. The desert and Islam bring torment to this place, the compelling torment that human words cannot adequately express . . .

The animal hasn't left. Anxious about my presence, it slinks, slinks amongst the tombs, keeping down low. It continues to yap because I have disturbed it. Long howls of an extremely high pitch issue from the mournful gullet of this scavenger of cadavers . . .

❖ ❖ ❖

HOWEVER, I FINALLY see my tents, looking like off-white cones among the village's vague walls of reddish mud. Since this cemetery has only one entrance, I decide I have to climb the wall. The wall of pebbles and dried earth gives way under my weight, and with a cloud of dust and a crumbling noise, it falls and makes a breach two or three meters long.—I hear it as I run as fast as I can, for fear some Bedouin might come, angry about this intrusion, to punish the profaner . . .

❖ ❖ ❖

IN THE CAMP ALL our people are up, domestics, cooks, interpreter, in extreme agitation and despair: the Bedouin from the Petraean desert have just arrived with our camels. They woke all our people up at sword's point after midnight to insist upon a meal from our best provisions, even inviting all the hungry prowlers to the party:

"They are devils! Devils! All devils!" our men say, and they prepare a meal with murder in their hearts, lighting big fires to roast our chickens and sheep.

Being robbed, pillaged, bilked—this was all foreseen. As long as they don't attack us personally, we have to let them have their way. We go off quietly to bed, forcing very friendly smiles to wish everyone a nice meal . . .

TWENTY-SEVEN

❖ ❖ ❖   *Thursday, March 15*

THUMP, THUMP, THUMP! Thump, thump, thump! . . . At the crisp coolness of three o'clock in the morning, the little wooden drum is again sending its slow and hollow beat down the dark oasis pathways. . . . It even goes around our camp, to inform the followers of Mohammed among us that today is another day of fasting.

It's too soon for me to wake up, because I went to sleep so late. I start to think about the hard day we face and about the very difficult farewells, now that we are in the hands of these unknown Bedouin and using the camels of my new friend, "who perhaps won't only have any robe on his face!"

As soon as the sun is up, our camp is circled by a raucous, shouting crowd. They are the camel drivers that we requested of Mohammed-Jahl, and a lot of totally worthless characters who followed the great bandit hoping to steal something from us. Under the silk couffies and woolen veils, we can see shadowy faces and the shine of malevolent eyes. In all directions, yellow and red metal glints from the excited groups. These men are armed with amulets and weapons, packs containing mysterious papers, long thin rifles used in desert escapades, long cutlasses notched by father, then son, to record their kills of man and beast.

The loudest yelling is near the tent containing our provisions. There is a circle of men sitting there, surrounded by a circle of men standing, and everybody is arguing ferociously. Right in the face of the others, they strike their own arms, clap their hands, or slap their own foreheads to increase the effect of their death threats.

In the middle of it all, I catch sight of Mohammed-Jahl, holding his riding crop as if it were a scepter, his eyes flashing with rage from under his beautiful veil tied with gold cords. He is roaring like a lion, old but still frightening and in charge. These people in rags around him are officials of his territory; he shares our fees with them, keeping the majority of the money for himself. So gold coins can be seen to pass five or six times from one to the other, clenched over and over by hands grabbing like claws.

Also the Arabs of Aqaba who served us as night guards form a tight group around our interpreter, demanding exorbitant sums for their three nights of duty. There are others with other demands: the one who lent his camel day before yesterday for the trip to Petra, and the one who wrote the letter to the great sheik, and the one who filled our water containers . . . Then new ones arrive constantly, this one wanting to sell a sheep, that one to sell a hen; they do it insistently, with rifle in hand, quoting prices on the outrageous level of a city under siege. As this all continues, they press closer and closer against our men, tugging on their clothes as if to tear them off.

Time goes by. Nothing is resolved. And our gold coins melt away.

The Turkish soldiers could have helped us a little this morning, but not one of them stirred from the citadel. And the caimacam, whose signature we are anxiously awaiting for right of passage, well—he's asleep! We are in Ramadan. The fasting and prayers have worn him out. He is laid out in his little thatch-roofed house, and his guards don't dare disturb his rest.

As for our camels, they look like dead animals, lying on their sides in poses of total exhaustion, with their long necks stretched out on the sand. Our guide has felt them and states unequivocally that they have not eaten for a week and will find it very difficult to travel today.

We are left out of this, and all attacks are directed at our men. However, the dark-faced group of hungry people continues to grow in number, and the volume of racket gets out of hand.

Only once did a group push too close to me (and I was trying to remain calm with a smile under my woolen veils). Mohammed-Jahl roared in with his stick raised. Using only one furious and brief order, he broke up the circle, and then he took my hand with a lordly grace and ushered me away as calmly as you please, to have me select my camel. However, he chooses for me, to make sure I have an excellent animal. He examines all the camels and tries my saddle and rifle on several different ones. I was hoping for a white camel, which seemed sharp and clean to me, but he rejects it with a disdainful shrug of the shoulders. His choice is a young male, which they get to stand with hearty blows of the whip. Of course I will ride this one: he is so slender, with such delicate legs and neck that he resembles an ostrich. He is truly elegant, as handsome as a camel can get. He is desert-color, a neutral warm gray with a touch of pink like everything else. He blends so well that one could say he has no color at all.

A searing and splendid sun lights the oasis and brightens the erstwhile square that was so noisy this morning and where we were camped. Through the curtain of palms can be seen the Prussian blue streak of the sea, laced with thin gray stems as if you were seeing it behind a screen of reeds. Our tents, our rugs, our saddles, and our baggage are scattered over the sand. The shouting men, these thin men with long rifles and cutlasses, stamp through it all, waving their arms wide in exasperation. There are also some packs of dogs, sheep, and goats. And all the children of Aqaba, funny little kids, some naked, others wearing burnouses too large for them and which drag in the sand, their faces and eyes covered with flies. Some of them are adorable even so, in physique and dark stares, with muscles like pagan statues. And the khamsin blows. And down on the excited crowd, on the rags, on the shining metal of the weapons, on the cries, the gestures, the greed, and the threats— great swarms of yellow grasshoppers strike like hailstones . . .

❖ ❖ ❖

IT SEEMS THE caimacam is now awake. He hasn't changed his mind while asleep, Allah be praised, and he confirms that we have permission to head for Palestine. Over in his old house at the corner of the little path with mud walls, the proper papers and contracts with Mohammed-Jahl are being slowly transcribed into Arabic.

The loading of our camels has begun. But it is easy to see that this will be slow: ten times, when one animal is loaded and ready to go, some wild-eyed armed character gnashing his teeth leaps in, and uttering curses he throws everything on the ground.

I can follow Mohammed-Jahl most of the time because of his stick raised above the crowds, but occasionally he pounces upon me like a battering ram. He wants me to be a witness to some horrendous thing committed by our guide: he tried to reduce the caravan by one camel to save money; or he welched on the price of a sheep; or else he hasn't given somebody the promised price. Every time this happens, I have to follow the old sheik to the location of the dispute . . . However, whenever he speaks to me directly, his gaze and his gestures immediately soften. Holding my hand in his very small hand, it is gently and with a great deal of courtesy that he leads me around . . .

❖ ❖ ❖

AT LONG, LONG LAST it is done, settled and signed. Everybody agrees now.

My traveling companions are already mounted; but as I get set to mount my steed with the birdlike legs, I get the message that the great sheik needs to speak with me again.

So I retrace my steps and look for him in the crowd. I had really intended to say good-bye to him anyway. At the end of the square, there he is, coming out of the caimacam's little pathway, very excited, furious, and looking daggers. Two other old men, one on each side of him, are holding hands with him. They are two old sheiks who are magnificent in their bearing and anger, as they skim along in their swirling clothes. All three are yelling at the same time and come on like a military charge; they seem to be a swarm of furies, slicing through this scorching wind, which whips their burnouses and veils into the air. Behind them other people are running, and they are somewhat scary, considering their menacing fever pitch . . . What is up now? What do they want of me? . . .

Luckily this new attack isn't against me, and I'm out of it.

On the contrary, as soon as they see me, they all stop and the face of the great highwayman calms down:

"Ah!" he says; "I wanted to tell you that I'm giving you my son Hassan, here he is (he pushes the old men aside and leads the young sheik forward by the hand), as your companion to Palestine. Listen, you came recommended to me. Well, now it's my turn to recommend my son Hassan to you."

I take Hassan by the shoulders and according to desert etiquette I lean his forehead against mine. Mohammed immediately does likewise with me, and this is a friendship pact sealed forever between us, a fact approved by a murmur from the crowd.

❖ ❖ ❖

NOW WE ARE ALL mounted, ready to leave at last.

It appears they are happy with us, with our gifts and our attitudes, because farewells and safe journeys are uttered by a crowd suddenly calm. We slowly depart, passing through the last little mud walls, the last palms of the oasis, relieved to have silence bit by bit and happy to have escaped that horde without leaving our clothes, our last piece of money, or our heads. It will soon be ten o'clock. Our departure took three difficult and possibly disastrous hours.

We move ahead in disorder, separated right away and alone in the sand and on the spindly desert brush. It seems a long time since we said farewell to the palm trees and their shade. And the sparkling sand is littered with those same yellow grasshoppers that fell like clouds upon Aqaba this morning.

A smiling man catches up with me and rides along beside me. He extends his arm and we shake hands over the gap between our camels. This is my new friend, the young Sheik of Petra, whom Mohammed-Jahl has delegated as our companion to Palestine.

He's nothing like his father. He's shorter, thinner, almost skinny, with his waist held by an overly tight leather belt. He's

twenty to twenty-five years old, very tan, with delicate face and features framed by a thin black beard. He is unusual and ugly, but
even so he has a certain charm that is almost feminine. He is as
gentle and retiring as his father is blustery. However, he is a bandit
like his ancestors and a killer on occasion. He has attractive
weapons and amulets. And like all the people in his tribe, he wears
long pointed sleeves that drag on the ground when he walks and
that float in the wind when he rides. He is mounted on a camel
somewhat like mine, with long marsh-fowl legs. He drives his animal with obvious pretense, but at least he does it with grace. In re-
sponse to the black wool reins, the startled beast rears and twists its
long snake-like neck into a strange position. Then it leaps about
like a big four-legged ostrich and gets entangled in the mass of
fringes and pendants hanging from its head down along its chest to
its flat hooves. Mounted high on its back, the young slender sheik
leans his delicate head as if under the weight of a very heavy veil
and regally holds in his hand straight ahead the traditional stick
whose shape suggests fresh lotus leaves that have not yet opened.

❖ ❖ ❖

WE GO ON. Soon the oasis is but a green line at the foot of the pink
granite rocks of Arabia. And the sea itself becomes a line, narrowing, narrowing, still its indescribable blue—then disappears completely. We are again passing through ash valleys and mountains, in
their uniform gray and pink desolation.

At times we pass dark holes that seem to go straight through
the rocks. In front of them are piles of bones. These are panthers'
lairs. No doubt they are sleeping at this time of day, but no doubt
they are also aware of our presence and half-open their yellow eyes.

It is oppressively hot, and more than that, it is dark. But the familiar peace of the desert seems delightful to us following the upset
and anxieties of Aqaba.

Our caravan is three men larger by the Turkish officer and the
two soldiers selected by the caimacam. They are dressed as

Bedouin. In addition we have five or six native travelers from the
northern tribes. They are strangers to us, but at the last moment
they had asked whether they could join us for their own safety.

How different our escort people are from those innocuous,
measly drivers we had rented in Suez. The new ones seem less
wretched, handsomer and stronger. They look fiercer, too, and
more determined. In retrospect it now seems that Aqaba is the authentic threshold of the desert . . .

❖ ❖ ❖

WE PROCEED AT a slow Ramadan pace. The men are tired because of
religious self-denials, and our animals are tired because of the
forced fasting and long distances covered since Aqaba. So we won't
make too much headway today, but we can catch up later. *In-chal-
lah!* After eleven days of crossing the Tih desert, we'll arrive in
Judea.

❖ ❖ ❖

OUR NIGHT CAMP is in the mountains, in one of those deep granite
gorges with perpendicular walls, where caravans like to stop because of the shelter against strong winds. Here one can also have
the illusion of being protected from nocturnal surprises.

High up between the rocks, in the slice of visible sky, the seven
stars of David's chariot have taken fire. And the Ramadan moon is
at the zenith, a half-disk of bright silver. Night, always marvelous,
has just come down on us with extremely transparent gaps and
some astonishingly sharp visions, all mixed with dreamlike
smudges.

Our whole caravan is resting. The men are sitting in little select
groups around fires. The Turks together. Over here, Bedouin from
Petra. Elsewhere, our Syrian Arabs. And off by themselves, our
four strangers. And around thirty camels dozing on their knees
among the men.

Some groups are very near and some are far away, dispersed all the way from the entrance of the dark corridors we used to get here. There are also upward steps of different heights on incredibly flat rocks—and our leaping flames light the dark faces, the white teeth, the shining sabers, the long burnouses, the majestic poses, and the monkey hunkering and jumble of naked arms and legs.

This is the day for baking the week's bread under coals—unleavened bread hard as a rock. This requires much bigger fires than usual, magnificent fires of fragrant branches.

For making the bread, such hot fires are needed, with flames so high and red that all the stone above seems on fire. The granite rises, the color of coals, into a sky that was glowing a little while ago, but which is at present almost a contrasting starless black—this makes a kind of shadowy hole, to the bottom of which a paler blue dying moon has slowly drifted, slowly drifted.

The virginal air we found in this lonely spot is being replaced by a complex Bedouin smell composed of camel musk, the animal smell of men, the perfume of Turkish pipes, and the perfume of burning fragrant branches.

❖ ❖ ❖

NOW THE BREAD IS baked and the fires are dying down. So the granite rocks also extinguish and blacken, while the pale moon regains its gold and silver colors. A sudden change in the world, another fantasy to please our eyes, which a healthful fatigue will soon close.

Some cicadas off in the spindly bushes and stunted little plants sing us a song of springtime, music we are hearing in Arabia for the first time.

Since it is the hour of prayer before bed, they are all up, the men, Bedouin from Petra and other Bedouin, turning toward Mecca, not so far away, to begin invoking the God of the deserts— then the real world retreats before the grandeur and the majesty of this prayer, surrounded by these rocks where moonbeams are descending . . .

TWENTY-EIGHT

❖ ❖ ❖ *Friday, March 16*

TODAY WHEN WE have crossed the mountains at whose foot we camped yesterday evening, we will enter the largest desert of Tih. Its expanses, so our drivers say, are immense and flat like the sea, a sea created by the play of incessant mirages.

We have the following information about the inhabitants of this desert, given by Isambert and Chauvet in their *Itinerary in Petraean Arabia*:

"The Arabs who occupy the desert of Tih count among the wildest and most intractable of the Bedouin. They are all plunderers and their raids, like those of the Amalekites, extend as far as the Syrian desert, in the area of Palmyra."

The Amalekites in fact, against whom the Hebrews waged so many battles, were the ancestors of the few tribes we will see on our route. They probably still resemble them, in face, costumes, and bearing, for nothing has changed in this land, the East made eternal in its dream and its dust.

❖ ❖ ❖

THUS WE HAVE TO begin this morning by climbing over the top of the Djebel-Tih mountain range, to reach the desert of the Amalekites on the other side.

The slopes are very steep for our burdened camels, and the cliffs under our feet get gradually steeper.

To our great surprise, here is a kind of road, which winds toward the desolate peaks and which rough boulders of rock arranged by man divide from the abyss below. Over a dry streambed there is even a bridge—a rough, rudimentary bridge, it is true, with a single massive arch—but improbable and totally unexpected here. In this country where the oldest things are pre-served in a special way and where the few new things take in their turn the uniform ash patina of the past, it is impossible to determine the age of this bridge. Was it Baudoin the First, king of Jerusalem, who had it built when he conquered Aelana, today the primitive Aqaba—or else King Solomon, when he came to this same Aelana, which was called Ezion-gaber then, to receive the beautiful visiting queen? No, this arch of stones, so it seems, is only twenty to thirty years old. Modern Arabs decided to build it at the same time as this makeshift road, because all the pilgrims from the west and north used it on their way to Mecca. Their caravans could really no longer cross these mountains, which were increasingly crumbly and rough.

In the gorges through which we climb, there is no green nature at all, but instead there is a great number of stones, a mighty and somber display of geological oddities. This morning we are in a mass of flesh-colored sandstone, *arborized* like the most precious agates. From all their recent cracks grow delicate black leaves, like ferns or maidenhair. They grow by the thousands. The smallest boulder under the feet of our camels is decorated with these wispy silhouettes of plants.

❖ ❖ ❖

WE ARE GETTING close to the top. We can see behind us, as if air-borne, over the Arabian Desert. It unfolds its pink wilderness to the horizon, and to our right the desert of Petra and the dark moun-tains of the country of Edom disappear.

The sky is now covered with a veil, and finally toward noon a new expanse unfolds ahead, an expanse that is deeper and drearier than all the areas around. It is a high region that is flush with the peaks we have just climbed and that nestles in the mysterious clouds. It is something like a sea, rising higher than all the sur-rounding territory. And it seems it could have congealed in a period of calm weather, leaving it eternally smooth and waveless: this is the desert of Tih, the desert of the Amalekites.

On the first plateaux we see hints of tracks, left by the time-honored passing of caravans. The tracks fade in the distance, tracks as numerous as the loomed threads of weavers. They group into two networks, one going west, the other north. The first indicates the route of believers from Egypt and the Maghreb; the second, which we are taking, is the route of pilgrims from Palestine and Syria.

This frightening crossroads of the desert sees crowds of twenty to thirty thousand people each year on their way to holy Mecca. But today it is barren, barren as far as the eye can see, and its mournful size and desolation seem frozen under a darkening sky. It is the usual stopping place of the multitudes and is littered with graves, like little menhirs of rough stones standing in pairs—one at the head, the other at the foot—places where pious pilgrim-travelers sleep.

❖ ❖ ❖

EXCITED BY ALL THIS space, our camels raise their heads, sniff the wind, and change their slow pace into something like a race.

This area is mud-gray. It is as flat as if someone had dragged giant rollers over it. Beyond the extent of our vision it is the same, and it is dark, under an even darker sky. There is a barely visible shine of moisture, despite the fact that its immense surface is totally composed of dried mud, parched, and with a thousand hairline fractures, like crazed porcelain.

Along the tracks our drivers stoop to pick up numerous very tiny stones the color of turquoise, which seem dazzling on the dirty gray of the ground. These are pieces of the beads that usually adorn camels' heads. From time immemorial these same paths have been used by caravans, so the fashion of this jewelry must go back three to four thousand years. The pieces of glass beads that we are collecting and that seem to be polished fossils could easily go back to the time of Moses or Solomon. It is strange to see these small, blue, almost eternal things that fell one by one over the years, finally marking the trail on these endless paths like Tom Thumb's crumbs of bread.

❖ ❖ ❖

AS WE CROSS THIS new wilderness, we are aware of the altitude, because the mountain peaks we left behind are all that rises above the horizon; they make a faint jagged outline, which is black now under the thick shadow of the clouds.

A very strange roof has formed above us, seemingly very near: Flakes of gray cotton that seem truly solid and that you could seemingly catch if you reached up a bit. And one could even say that in many places, hands have stretched out these tufts toward the earth, to spin them on bobbins. Here and there some tufts of a darker gray hang down, but in a way to suggest that someone has held and twisted them by hand—and it causes a vague unexplainable chill, as any strange occurrence in the sky does.

We are making some speed now. Our camels are completely alert and are lengthening the stride of their thin legs. They point their long birdlike necks into the cooler wind of the altitude. From time to time, through a hole in the clouds, an unexpected ray falls on us. It casts our shadows oddly and then snuffs out, leaving us in a gloomier diffuse light.

On these plains of cracked mud, which are as flat as spread-out cloth, we can appreciate better the vulnerability of man and beast, the roughness of the silhouettes, the antiquity of posture and dress. Our new caravan moves, moves faster because it is much less encumbered than the last one, but also even more unencumbered because it is moving through open space, endless space, the same space all around as far as the eye can see. Thin animals, thin men, bodies thinned by desert fasting, but muscular, muscular with strength and grace. The animals have a nervous step that goes and goes in spite of their usual hunger. The men have bare arms and legs like works of bronze metal sticking out of burnouses. Rifles and cutlasses bump together with dry clicks. Tufts of black hair sway and dance. Tooled leather wrapped around narrow waists. Amulets and pendants . . .

❖ ❖ ❖

A BRIEF CONVERSATION with my new driver:
   "Is your homeland far?" he asks.
   "Oh yes, it is very far."
   "Is it Beirut? Or Cham (Damascus)?"
   "No, much farther. It's on the other side of the Great Sea."
   A silence while he ponders this, then he raises astonished eyes to me:
   "The other side of the Great Sea? But how can you cross the sea? You can't walk on water."
   He is a Bedouin from Petra, and all he knows is the Aqaba Sea, which has no boats. I try to explain to him: planks that float.
   "But what makes your planks move?"
   Quickly his incredulous mind is no longer interested, and silence again reigns.
   Around our groups, which are spread out like lost souls in nothingness, nothing happens, nothing changes, and nothing exists. Countless hours roll by. We are simply moving in the vast sweep of nature.
   Once we see a snake, wiggling on the smooth ground as it crosses our path. Then our shouting drivers kill it. This is a fleeting moment of astonishing noise, but it is soon over, drowned and forgotten in the great calm of our silent steady movement ahead.
   It is as if we were being carried off on high boats, gently rocking, which seem to be crossing a somber sea with invisible shores.

❖ ❖ ❖

BUT AT EVENING, while our tents are being pitched and we are making camp in the vastness, over there, yonder, a small human group, bristling with rifles, begins to appear from the depths of the flat horizon.

Sheik Hassan, his hand shading his eyes to see better, takes on an expression of suspicion:

"They are on foot," he says; "they don't have any camels, nor any tents, nor any women. They are *desert bandits*!"

TWENTY-NINE

❖ ❖ ❖

H OWEVER, THEY APPROACH at an unthreatening gait, and we size
each other up. They look mean and are half-naked under
rags. They are almost all young, looking sturdy despite their extreme thinness, and they are noble in attitude and shape. But they
have faces of poor starving wolves, with expressions of cruelty and
suffering. There are around thirty of them and twenty-five of us. In
addition we have three repeating rifles. The fight would at least be
even, and they must think so, too, because as they arrive they greet
us and bow warily and sit down on the ground, where they act as if
they were intending to go to sleep for the night.

We ask them: "What do you want from us?"

"Oh, nothing," they say. "Only we are afraid of being alone out
here *because there are bandits*! So we'll take advantage of your company until tomorrow morning."

Afraid of being alone! They have nothing anybody would
want to steal, and there are thirty-six of them armed to the teeth.
Our reply is an ultimatum of war:

"Leave immediately. Get out of our sight before nightfall. If
you don't we'll shoot you!"

A minute of hesitation and ugly sneers. Then they get up, collect their sorry rags and their sorry bags, and leave like whipped
dogs.

We pity them. We would have given them something to eat,
even if they are robbers, but we don't have an oversupply, because
our people from Petra, improvident as birds, brought only enough
barley meal for the bread of the first days out, and no drinking
water, and we will be obliged to provide for them all the way to
Palestine.

❖ ❖ ❖

THE AWNING OF DARK clouds that had been overhead during the day has lifted slightly, detached from the horizon to the west. The setting sun, enormous and red, has descended down low into this narrow opening, right on the edge of the earth.

However, the little group bristling with rifles is now reaching the far distance rapidly. They are now pygmies, these desert thieves, and then they are lost in the far reaches of this flat expanse. "It's a trick. They will come back tonight!" says Hassan, as he watches them disappear . . .

Now half the sun has sunk behind the desert. Only half of its red fiery disk can be seen, as happens at sea on evenings of calm. But its rays have enough strength yet to cast our shadows, which are long parallel rays, endless rays across the plain. A big white female camel is the only one standing in the whole caravan, and her body is outlined with an aura of gold. She seems a giant beast in silhouette against the dying light. She bellows a long sad cry at the sinking sun in its full splendor. Perhaps she is feeling some elemental sadness, some indefinable kind of contemplation . . .

Then night falls. We can just barely see the vast black circle of the expanses around us. In the middle of it our watch fires suddenly ignite, with the crackling of a conflagration.

❖ ❖ ❖

WHILE WE WERE eating in the tent, the clouds evaporated, melting into the sky with the swiftness characteristic of this country where rain cannot fall.

The half-moon of Ramadan spills onto the desert a resplendent light that is somehow mysterious. In the middle of a dark blue sky where occasional white tufts race along, it is very high, at the zenith, practically erasing our earthly shadows, making us appear to each other in the white and frozen pose of ghosts.

At this delightful hour, when you chat and dream, sitting before your light cloth lodgings, a group such as we would apparently gather every night forms at the entrance to my tent, around coffee and cigarettes. There is the Turkish officer who accompanies us. There is the little Sheik Hassan. His cousin Aït, sheik of the drivers. And the one of the five unknown travelers who seemed to us a person of quality, worthy of sitting in our company.

All familiar with this desert, they are preoccupied with the prowlers and expect an attack from them during the night. We agree to take turns on watch and to have our weapons ready. We also agree to have sentinels posted on all four sides.

Then we chat and we begin to know each other.

The Turkish officer is from Baghdad, an old hand at spending his life in wasteland assignments.

The unknown traveler, whose name is Brahim, is a sheik from a northern tribe, rich in cattle, *a prince of Kedar* (*Isaiah* LX:7; *Ezekiel* XXVII:21). He has just spent four years as captive of a southern sheik more powerful than he is, as punishment for the robbery and murder he had committed on his territory. He is returning home with four faithful servants. He is an old man with a gray beard, whose symmetrical and hard face almost disappears under the hanging folds of a pilgrimage veil.

Aït, the son of one of Mohammed-Jahl's brothers—an exquisite delicate face, white porcelain teeth, and over each ear three braids of hair in the old style—tells us he is twenty-five, that he is married and the father of two little nomads.

Sheik Hassan, who is scarcely twenty himself, tells us that his first wife was Aït's sister, his cousin, but that he repudiated her because she wasn't giving him children. With his second wife he has just had a little girl . . .

While we are talking, one of our drivers passes near me. He is wearing on a shoulder strap an arsenal of things that shine in the moonlight: powder flasks, flint, Turkish pipe pincers, all the accessories fitting for an elegant Bedouin. I stop him and offer to buy all this from him to complete my outfit. At this Hassan, who has been searching for ways to please me, takes it from the man and gives it to me.

❖ ❖ ❖

ONE O'CLOCK in the morning. We were asleep under the resplendent white of the moon, very quiet in this immense quiet.

Suddenly the silence is broken, a loud savage cry! Gunshots! Bang! bang! bang! . . . Then a confusion of noise, war cries, cries of rage and fright, falsetto voices that screech "to the death!" . . .

Through my raised door, I see all our Bedouin running, maniacal, in the same direction, half-naked, with nightshirts flapping, like a flock of big birds dispersed by flying lead . . . Senseless activity, however, for we can't tell whom to aim at. We're half-asleep yet and are somewhat blinded by moonbeams . . .

All we can see is a confused bunch of people over there, and we can't recognize anybody . . . We stay here, though, riveted to the spot by the instinct of guarding our precious supplies, and keeping our three Syrians close by . . .

❖ ❖ ❖

THE FIRING STOPS, the yelling dies down, and calm again takes over. The excited sentries rush back to camp. The whole fracas took only three short minutes . . .

Now they are all back, still very excited and all talking at once.

"What happened?" we ask. "Is it over?"

Our sentries to the south saw men approaching on the run. As soon as they sounded the alarm, they say, these bandits fired on them. But now they have fled, because they saw we were well guarded. Then they disappeared into the dark.

Good Heavens. That story is quite possible. But perhaps, too, the sentries may have dreamed it all, or fired at vague shadows, as much through fright as to give themselves the honor and illusion of a little war. We will never know the truth. What is certain is that nobody in our group is wounded. The only one shedding a little blood states that he got entangled in his own saber.

More and more skeptical as we think about it, we tell our Bedouin that if we are attacked again, they shouldn't get too close to the enemy, for we would be shooting at random into the bunch with repeating rifles.

Then we fall into a deep sleep until daytime.

THIRTY

❖ ❖ ❖ *Saturday, March 17*

THE SAME CURTAIN of gray tufts that covered us yesterday covers us again at dawn, after the setting of the moon. We awaken under a sky of funereal black.

We set off again to the north, in this desert of a yellowish gray that seems to be just *expanse*, expanse in its most elemental form, but also the most exciting kind to cross. The wind, which blows almost cold under this great shroud of clouds, stimulates life and pushes with such rapid force that we have never felt so intoxicated with space and emptiness.

The desert is now uniform and smooth. In the distance, however, under heavy slow-moving clouds, waves begin to appear, like a rising tide on a motionless sea.

Scaly lizards, the same color as the ground and the whole area, cross our caravan in a steady stream, under the feet of our camels.

Occasionally there is a scrawny violet flower, which the camels love to eat. With a little contented cry, when they come upon the flowers, they tug on their reins of black wool and stretch their long necks toward the ground.

This morning we left behind on our right the trail of the Syrian pilgrims. And now we have no track to follow, no trail to show us the way.

❖ ❖ ❖

AFTER THE FIRST two hours of travel, the expanse changes colors. The desert, from the yellowish that it was, becomes black ahead of us. We had already experienced those colors, but less accented, less somber. There is first a transitional zone that is marbled and crossed with great black and yellow stripes. Then we go into absolute black.

This black is only on the surface. It is an inexplicable layer of pebbles that seem to be onyx. They look as if they had fallen like hail from the sky. One could say that someone has taken care to equalize their sizes and to preserve them, in such a way as to spread as few of them as possible over countless leagues. Just underneath is sand, and the feet of our camels cut through this thin black layer, leaving yellow tracks on the desert.

❖ ❖ ❖

THIS MORNING THE young Sheik of Petra, not finding my saddle luxurious enough, gave me his—and now a dozen long black pendants hang down on each side of my camel's flanks, almost dragging on the ground when my pace or the wind don't blow them around.

My driver Abdul, in spite of his very fierce appearance, is also very giving and kind with me, showing me a broad range of childish attentions. He collects, as gifts for me, the blue glass beads that continue to litter the ground, as well as the sorry flowers that grow in our way.

❖ ❖ ❖

ABOUT TEN O'CLOCK in the morning, still no rain. But the clouds dissipate mysteriously. In the blink of an eye, the roof of the sky, which was so low and threatening, melts away in all directions at the same time. And the sun reappears, shining abruptly and hot abruptly, too. The wind that blew so cold through our clothing down to the skin becomes a warm caress.

Then the brush reappears. Not the brush of the south, not the delicious myrrh that we miss, nor the unknown plant that filled the desert with a green-apple perfume, but thornbush and hyssop.

❖ ❖ ❖

SHEIK BRAHIM, who also swamps me with his gifts, has his camel kneel and insists that I ride it for the day. "A marvelous animal," he says, "and it would please me immensely."

Indeed, a very small and slim animal, which trots without shaking, like a fast horse or a gazelle. Instead of a monumental saddle like mine, he has on his back just a simple switch of tooled leather, decorated with beads and shells. As soon as I touch him at the base of the neck with my lotus-leaf stick, I'm off like an arrow, at a light trot ahead of the caravan . . .

Right away little Sheik Hassan catches up with me and insists that his camel is far superior, and he wishes I would try it also. So we change, to please him, and we continue to trot side by side, moving ahead into the monotonous expanse and losing sight of the slower caravan behind.

A burning day follows the dark morning. The sun climbs in a sky now completely blue. The flat land in the distance trembles with heat, and the empty distant land seems to be preparing for all kinds of visions and mirages . . .

"*Gazal! Gazal!*" (gazelles!) Sheik Hassan shouts, as we are tramping on the scraggly bushes . . .

Indeed, going in the opposite direction from us, they pass like a cloud of sand. They are delicate little animals, fast little skittish beasts . . . But the wobbling and turbulent lands in the distance distort them and make them vanish from our baffled gaze.

We stay far ahead, trotting and halting.

At about eleven o'clock the first nonexistent lake appears, and we are both fooled. It seemed like very blue water with the reflections of trees, trees that were only the magnified images of spindly desert bushes . . .

Soon there are lakes with tempting water all around. They distort, change, overflow, disappear, and return. Great lakes or rivers that meander or just pools that reflect imaginary reeds . . .

There are still more of them. It's like a sea that might engulf us little by little, a disturbing sea that shimmers . . .

But around noon this whole blue fantasy disappears in just two or three minutes, as if we had snuffed it out. Now nothing but dry sand. Now the land of thirst and death is upon us, real and unrelenting.

❖ ❖ ❖

WE WANT TO lay over tonight in a place called the Oued-Gherafeh, where there is water—real water renowned in the Tih desert—so we arrive at the campground early.

As soon as we have set foot on the ground by our set-up tents, the young Sheik of Petra takes my hand to show me this precious water.

I was expecting a beautiful rushing spring. But it is a pond only three meters long, in sand and mud. They have already drawn our water, and now it's the turn of our camels and drivers. They all get in knee-deep, and the animals, drinking with the men, drop their musky dung into the pond.

Around the camp there are shrubs of some size, thorny locusts, bushes with off-white flowers, all nourished by being near this pond. And that makes this place attractive for ambushes, for night attacks, for thieves who hide and creep. Moreover it is not our custom to camp among large bushes, with some distance to travel for water at the source. Into this somewhat gloomy grove, lost in the vast stretches of desert and lit by the five o'clock light, we have brought a kind of country life—while above our heads swirls a jumbled black cloud of migratory birds. They were no doubt on their way north for spring and had intended to stop here for water if we hadn't been around.

❖ ❖ ❖

TOWARD SUNSET LEO comes and tells me of his remorse about having killed a poor owl in the brush near the pond. I must say that we both have tender feelings for hoot owls and horned owls. Besides, killing for the pleasure of killing has always seemed to us an indication of animal mentality—and the Western idiots who without necessity and without peril *have a good time* destroying sparrows and quail have no excuse, so far as we are concerned . . .

But he was pressured and distracted. The Arabs were pointing out the bird off in the distance, saying: "Shoot!" And hurriedly, without recognizing the friendly species and perhaps to show off the accuracy of his weapon, he fired . . .

"Suppose we buried him," he suggests; "that would be best."

On the sand, near the water hole, lies the poor owl. It was a superb animal, in the prime of its youth, with very smooth plumage. It is still warm, and its large yellow eyes, fixed open, stare at us with the very intelligent sadness of a cat.

We dig a little trench in the sand.

When the owl is in the hole on its back, with its wings hugging its body like a monk's cloak, it still stares at us obstinately, with an astonished expression of reproach that cuts us to the quick.

On the poor yellow eyes which will never be seen again, on the so well-groomed and beautiful feathers that will soon rot, we throw sand. Then we roll a heavy rock over to assure peace for this tomb . . .

Rather childish, I admit, these two Bedouin burying an owl so piously, deep in the solitudes of the Tih desert, as the great golden sun is sinking and flaming out . . .

❖ ❖ ❖

SINCE HASSAN PREDICTS a night attack, we take our battle stations by the light of the moon, giving assignments to our Bedouin, the Turkish officer included. We also made a blockhouse with three boxes. At heart I think we are dying to be attacked, because the mock battle of last night, the war cries and shooting in the empty wastes, have been unique and unforgettable.

Then we have the peaceful vigil by our tents. The Sheiks Hassan, Aït, and Brahim sit gravely in a circle with us in the beautiful white moonlight, to chat and smoke before bed. We hear stories of their raids and pillaging, which they tell us as easily as you please—and which we accept as easily, due to how far these latitudes alter human ways of seeing things . . . But suddenly, in the direction of the pond where the owl was killed, comes a faint little "Hoo! Hoo!" The call is both hushed and plaintive . . .

"Oh, fine," says Leo, "that's all we need, *the other one* calling for him now!"

The other one, you understand what we mean by *the other one*. *The other one* is its wife or husband. These birds are always in pairs. Probably the only couple for many leagues around, they had no doubt chosen these scrawny bushes by the water for a rendezvous tonight.

The other one keeps calling, "Hoo! Hoo!" We visualize again the reproachful expression in the two yellow eyes now buried in sand. And we forget the intriguing stories of bandits, we forget the hoped-for skirmish, and we forget anything that amused us, when we hear with a skip of our hearts the lonely cry of that poor bird . . .

THIRTY-ONE

❖ ❖ ❖ *Sunday, March 18 Palm Sunday*

No AMBUSH TONIGHT. But our camels have been restless. In the daylight this morning, we find on the sand around the camp the numerous and very fresh tracks of the prowlers that upset them: panthers!

We set off. Again it is the featureless desert, a circle of nothing, as flat and empty as a sea with no ships or shores. It draws a dark gray streak through the pale and clear sky. And more of this inexplicable film of black pebbles, as if little onyx hailstones had fallen.

The caravan moves on silently this morning. And we become pensive when confronted by the permanence of this absolute emptiness.

Nevertheless the horizons dim as the rising sun heats the desert. Then the extremely vague illusions of white muslin and reflecting vapors that precede mirages begin to shimmer in several directions at the same time.

Over there is a herd of large animals with long necks—white camels!—but in vast numbers. They move slowly in the light, which is both dazzling and hazy. They seem to be grazing . . . At any rate we don't trust our eyes, because we know that correct proportions don't exist in the desert when its fantastic sights are on display . . .

Oh! One of the camels unfolds broad wings and flies away!— Then two, then three—then all of them . . . Storks! It was really an incredible flock of storks that we scared off. They rise en masse, and others appearing out of nowhere join the group. They swirl through the air and black out the sky. We realize that this was yesterday evening's cloud.

No doubt all the storks of Europe are going back home for spring.

❖ ❖ ❖

WHEN THEY ARE GONE, we can see nothing but empty space.

But here are little undulations all around, like wavelets on a calm sea. They are dirty gray hills, very low and incredibly long. They are either parallel or they branch into arteries. They are accented by a brown or violet color along their highest ridges, like the darker shade of hair on the spine of animals.

Ten o'clock. Ten thirty. It was about this same time when the little fairyland lakes had begun to appear yesterday. Already a few materialize—so cool and so blue!—harbingers no doubt of a larger illusion to come. They still threaten to flood out and swamp you. But on the contrary, when you get close—blink! Nothing. The lakes are swallowed by the arid sand or folded up like blue cloth. Then they dissolve rapidly and in silence, like the imagined things they are.

❖ ❖ ❖

Then there passed by Midianites
merchantmen . . .

(*Genesis* XXXVII:28)

AROUND NOON, IN A place where there are a few bushes, we notice a lot of people and camels, very real this time.

These strangers approach us. They are wearing long robes, mostly pink or blue. They have attractive faces, whiter and fuller than those of the Bedouin. And there are a few blond beards. They approach with the customary ceremony, touching our heads with their turbans and making hospitable kisses in the air.

They are Arab merchants who seven days ago left Gaza (where we are headed) and who are going to the Aqaba oasis (that we have left behind). They make this trip every year to sell robes and burnouses to the desert tribes, as has been done since the time of the

Midianites. There are quite a few of these merchantmen, and they are well armed. Their camels are heavily loaded, and we have come across them at the right time, as we need to buy fresh clothing. In the blazing sunlight and on the sparkling pebbles, they unfold long-sleeved Bedouin shirts and white or black cloaks.

Then, after making our purchases, we say good-bye with wishes for safe passage. They go one way and we go the opposite. And our respective images begin to undulate. Soon their camels seem double because of the air. And they themselves, now elongated, now shortened, seem to have two heads apiece, like the kings and queens on decks of cards.

❖ ❖ ❖

BEYOND THE LITTLE hills come the plains. And beyond the flat plains come more little rolling hills. Wasteland after wasteland. And when you multiply in your mind's eye all the wastelands still to come, a vague feeling of terror comes over you.

❖ ❖ ❖

WE STOP FOR THE night in a strange place. It is a kind of deep amphitheater, an unusual crater in the plains we have crossed for three days.

The walls of this vast pit have folds and pleats like cloth stretched over stakes. They also have the same colors and streaks as desert things made from camel skin. So one could say we have camps of giant Bedouin around us, along with monstrous tents, stacked in two or three layers.

When the sun goes down, all these folded mountains take on dark colors, greenish yellow and burnt sienna. The whole picture is in startling sharpness, neatly cut from a somber sky the color of wine. It is like looking through an enormous ruby. Then the moon of Ramadan climbs into this cold and purplish-blue pink. The great full moon seemed at first like a pewter disk, almost touching the earth. And the whole scene becomes disorienting and frightening. Imagining yourself in past epochs, you could now believe you are seeing the climb of a dead satellite above a dead planet.

❖ ❖ ❖

NIGHT FALLS. A large bug the size of a bat comes and hums around our tents, flashing at times its little light of green phosphorus like a firefly.

And the large pewter disk suspended in the air changes into polished silver. Then it becomes white fire, then bluish fire, getting brighter and brighter and turning our resting caravan into statues, freezing and fixing everybody in their postures of rest. Meanwhile, in the direction of the sunset some time after nightfall, a gleam of daylight persists as a pink halo. How bright, how bright the moon, like a second sun—a somewhat phantom sun, it is true, whose rays spread cold and light and deathly quiet. But its pale splendor out-shines our smouldering fires. And when the sheiks, draped in their traditional veils, arrive slowly at my tent for the evening gathering, you could think you were seeing marble prophets conjured up in a magic glow.

THIRTY-TWO

❖ ❖ ❖ *Monday, March 19*

C AMP IS STRUCK. To leave the amphitheater where we slept, we climb up onto one of those things surrounding us in the form of superhuman tents. Then new wastelands appear, one after the other, in a glazed panorama, while the morning sun sketches our thin shadows over the cover of black pebbles.

Here and there on these new plains, we see more of those things that look like tents, but singly now. Some rise like plain pointed cones. Others have outrageous horns, as if the cloth were raised and stretched by hidden stakes. And they all are decorated with brown rays like Bedouin cloth.

Slowly they move farther behind, as the plains flatten and return to the condition of empty space where nothing can be seen.

Ten o'clock. It is the time for mirages. First we see a cool little river, which seems to call us, strangely, temptingly, with the reflection of trees in its floating water. Then, near and far the fragile deceptive lakes begin to play, roil, and expand. But it's no use: we don't fall for it any more.

❖ ❖ ❖

AROUND NOON WE pass a large nomad camp. We maintain a certain distance between their tents and our caravan. Their tents are similar in miniature to the hills of this morning, which are disappearing on the horizon behind us. They have the same shape, the same gradation of colors, and the same striped design. At this oppressive time of day, no one is visible there, but a large number of camels graze around, and guard dogs warn of our presence with frantic barking.

❖ ❖ ❖

IN THE BRIGHT light of three o'clock, we next pass a field of bushes. They are entirely covered with flowers that are off-white, a shining and almost metallic white.

In this kind of little silvery grove, the young Sheik of Petra goes ahead of us, because he's having problems with his disobedient camel. The high-strung young animal fights back, jumps like a wild goat, twists its swanlike neck, roars, and reaches back with bared teeth to bite. And it is finally subdued by its rider. Then they take off at a gazelle's gallop through the scrub, whipping these silvery bushes around with a mass of fringes, pendants, and black tassels. They are elegant and dainty silhouettes in flight on the desert horizon . . .

❖ ❖ ❖

WE CAMP TONIGHT in a place called Ouady-Loussein, where there is some greenery.

And here we receive the horrible visit of a mass of long-haired gray caterpillars, which arrive in militant, slow, and seemingly endless rows.

THIRTY-THREE

❖ ❖ ❖ *Tuesday, March 20*

I N THIS OUADY-LOUSSEIN ravine our camels have not slept well
again. They got up several times with grunts, no doubt because
of the skulking panthers. But our fires burned bright all night, to
discourage surprise attacks.

At sunrise we again take on our interminable journey to the
north. The light is bland. The setting, banal and dull. In just a few
hours, either we are getting tired of the desert or the desert is weary
of displaying its silent magic for us.

But at the end of the plateau we were crossing, new regions
suddenly appear, in an enormous unfolding all the way to the first
battlements of the Moab country. There is a clarity in the air that al-
lows us to see very faraway things. We see deserts of very shiny pale
sand, in a coloring we have not seen before. Chains of somber hills
that are also pale cross it, one after the other, like a series of vertebrae. Studied carefully they take on the same tentlike impression
that had struck us yesterday. They have points and horns, with
streaks of faded Bedouin cloth or panther coloring bleached by the
sun.

Emptiness and immensity had not yet been revealed to us in
this way, with such striking shades of white. We are really very far
from the land of pink granite where the myrrh was growing. Here
the expanse is set with relentlessly off-white, chalky coloring, which
the centuries have been able to barely tint with gold. On these dazzling plains, only a few of the bushes with white and gray flowers
grow; they are so laden with blooms that one could say they are
sprays of pewter or silver.

And suddenly here's a big, clear, shimmering blue lake that un-
dulates on a broad scale, reaches out and tumbles its water on the
western part of these forsaken lands.

128

There is a heavy, drowsy heat and, in the monotonous swaying of the camels, our eyes drift shut.

❖ ❖ ❖

"HAVE THE CAMELS PASSED?" It's the same question every day after our noon rest, when we are half-awake on the burning sand. Translation: "Has the whole group passed, the one including our pack camels? It has followed us all morning and is supposed to meet with us at the noon rest and precede us during the afternoon. Has it moved on? Is it time for us to remount and leave?"

"Yes, a half-hour or an hour ago," replies a Bedouin voice from somewhere.

"Let's go then! Bring the camels!" (*I allah, djib djimmel!*)

With your head still dreaming, you stretch and wake up. The dazzled eye first sees the tent, with its bold variegations of color, its white Arabic inscriptions on red, and its Persian rugs. Then, through the wide opening of the canvas, you see the dull sparkle of stones and sand and the shadow of a camel down on all fours in the sunlight.

The camels were grazing around in the hot wastes. Being obliged to come back and kneel, they complain with those cavernous raucous cries that are the most common noise the desert has to offer.

Once we are on our animals (which stood up in two stages), we have the impression of coolness because we are higher up, farther off the overheated ground. We look ahead very far in our intended direction, and we set off again, aiming at the monotonous wide-open spaces.

❖ ❖ ❖

MORE THAN THREE days now to reach Gaza, the Palestinian city closest to the wilderness of the south. And our Arabs say that already the desert will be less deserted, that already in the valleys we would find water here and there, and consequently herds and men.

At around two o'clock, on the slope of a pale hill with clothlike streaks, we begin to see series of long and dirty black things that are nestled on the ground like animals stuck there. They seem like a prodigious enlargement of the caterpillars at Ouady-Loussein. A powerful tribe is camped here, one of those tribes that are "rich in flocks" mentioned by the prophets.

The tents, very low as protection against the winds, are in long straight lines for three or four rows, spread out in limitless space. Countless herds are grazing around. Many female camels are nursing comical little newborns with long sheeplike wool not yet sheared, looking like both an ostrich and a lamb.

And black goats, black like polished ebony or jet, are grouped by the hundreds. In all directions they form stark blemishes on the white desert. The shepherds exchange greetings and air-kisses with us. The wary shepherdesses veil themselves more completely at our approach, and they seem to be ghosts as black as the goats they herd.

This is the tribe of the Sheik Brahim, who takes leave of us with many thanks, without asking us to rest in his tent, however. No doubt he is nervous about what he will find in his tent after such a long captivity.

Having left the Desert of Pharan, we are now entering the land of Kedar, with almost the same bad reputation in biblical times; and the prophets, indignant about the sins of Israel, shouted: "And send unto Kedar, and consider diligently, and see if there be such a thing!" (*Jeremiah* 11:10). The centuries have rolled by, and Kedar has remained a dark land of banditry and crime . . .

❖ ❖ ❖

THEN THE EXPANSE IS empty again until evening. And we camp in a place, still largely deserted, called Ouady-Caicire, deep in a valley, near a somewhat brackish spring in the sand.

The hills here have a vague green tint that we had never seen in Petraean Arabia until now. It is our first grass. The desolation of the earth is almost over. Around us there are reeds, grassy areas, and some flowers. Miniature flowers, it is true, but they are almost like flowers back home. Little irises standing scarcely two inches above the ground. Yellow tulips variegated with red, about as big as fingernails. Also tiny gillyflowers and microscopic carnations.

At the same time, the sky has become like the sky in the north: the moon, more hidden by mist, has been surrounded by a halo. Long cattail clouds drag through the sky, and the horizon is dark. Night comes mournful and veiled over this land of green.

Feeling the arrival of a more humid land's cold, our Bedouin put on their clothing of long-haired skins and wear winter-night head-gear, wrapping their heads and throats with a brown veil, whose two ends stick out on each side of the temple like long wild-rabbit ears.

❖ ❖ ❖

IN AMONG THE MANY tiny flowers, there grows a giant flower, a kind of yellow stem that comes leafless from a bulbous root.

Sheik Aït, roving around at the first blush of twilight, finds the largest of all and picks it for me as a gift. Like the other men, he has put on his tunic of goatskin and his rabbit-ear headgear. He smiles, showing teeth of an extraordinary white, as sharp as wolf's teeth. With his locks of hair, which fall along his primitive face, he has a strange and almost fantastic appearance in the door to my tent, in this desert of shadows, holding his large unknown flower in his hand.

❖ ❖ ❖

THE WATCH THIS TIME is accompanied by the song of owls. Some weird hoo-hoos come from all directions, from the darkness of bushes and the black valley depths. The hills blend with the clouds to form curtains of vague shadows around us. Our starting of fires makes the sudden nightfall seem darker. All we can see are men in their fur cloaks and long animal ears, squatting in silence around branches in flame.

THIRTY-FOUR

❖❖❖ *Wednesday, March 21*

How DIFFERENT THE atmosphere is already! It is no longer the pristine, sharp, and desiccating air that spread its shroud on a lifeless world of sand and stone. No, it is something less bitter perhaps, but infinitely less pure. In it one feels the weight of spring and the breath of meadows.

Aside from a herd of gazelles that scurries off in the morning, it is true that we come across nothing living for the eight to ten leagues of today's leg. These are still uninhabited expanses, but no longer the echoing deserts.

No more plays of light or mirages. And no more geological curiosities. The hills have ordinary forms now and familiar coloring, where green will soon reign.

The sky grows dim with water vapor, the breeze is soft, and the horizon is clouding over. We see more and more grass; and as the hours go by, we find it more abundant. By evening all the hills are green.

Doubtless this is only temporary. It is just an ephemeral veneer, created by March rain, and which the sun will burn off soon. And we sense an unexpected magic at the newness here, the same as we felt when the desert didn't change at all.

For the night we camp in a vast field, an endless expanse with no trace of humans anywhere, but fresh and enameled with flowering daisies and red poppies.

THIRTY-FIVE

❖ ❖ ❖   *Thursday, March 22*

Oppressive weather. Sky heavy and gray.

Our departure in flowering plains reminds us of past safaris between Meknes and Tangiers. These are not quite the fields of Morocco, with their magnificent range of colors, but already we have carpets of anemones, pink catchflies, white daisies, violet irises, and yellow marigolds.

Soon it will be Canaan, the land friendly to man, the *land of milk and honey*, instead of those resplendent forsaken solitudes we have left behind, and which barely sustain the underfed and thieving Bedouin.

❖ ❖ ❖

Around noon in a gardenlike valley, we came upon a poor sick camel, sitting beside a dead camel, whose belly had already been torn apart by wild animals. Some caravan abandoned it there to die. It tries to get up and to follow us, but it falls again after several steps, exhausted and done for, with its head in the grass.

❖ ❖ ❖

Everything seems to be softening, the light, shapes and colors. The hills no longer have contorted forms, but are gently rounded under a cloak of green. Mists hang in the distance and dilute the colors. It seems that all the earth's light has been transformed and muted.

Wonderful noons and nights occur only in lands where the air, deadly to plants, is free of water vapor and diaphanous as the universal void. Our memories of the desert we left behind are now like those one would keep upon returning to everyday reality after having seen almost terrifying magic.

Green, this new green, continues to intensify all around us. The asphodels that we found yesterday so star-shaped and short now grow taller and become more and more beautiful. There are enormous irises of a marvelous violet color. There are arums with black flowers that look like velvet trumpets. And tortoises crawl along the ground. And quail scatter in the high grass. Joyous larks soar through the sky, and the air bursts with birdsongs. Life rises, rises everywhere all at once, mesmerizes and overwhelms us, we travelers from the strange lands of death.

At night we come across the first fields sown by man, fields of barley, worked into rows and more wonderfully green than the preceding meadows.

And some Arabs, either shepherds or laborers whose tents are nearby, come to our camp in a friendly way to visit and sit with us around our fires.

THIRTY-SIX

❖ ❖ ❖ *Friday, March 23*

GOOD FRIDAY. We awaken to the singing of larks among plants and flowers in this immense green plain. The sky is spread with a pearl-gray veil, whose folds seem to hang down to the earth, and which might soon deliver a little rain.

We will enter Palestine this very day, the anniversary of the day (soon to be two thousand years ago), when the crucifixion took place of the Consoler whom man will never explain . . . And recalling Him is sufficient even today to convey an inexpressibly gentle magic to this land where His memory calls . . .

❖ ❖ ❖

RAIN, GRASS, AND wet grass—we had lost the habit of these things such a long time ago!

Then we hear women's voices, a sound also forgotten for so many days. Three Bedouin women straddling donkeys are going through the camp laughing; and they are not forbidding like those of the real desert. When they sit up to see us better, we see their dark blue veils, dotted with raindrops that look like eyes. Their faces are hidden under coral and silver netting, through which they watch us while the rest of it hangs over their throats in glittering pendants . . .

❖ ❖ ❖

ON WE GO THROUGH real pathways bordered with tulips, anemones, and asphodels; they are surrounded by barley fields that cover the plains with their magnificent velvet.

During the afternoon a crack appears in the flat land, and a

135

clear running river appears. We wade across, and on the other shore we are in Palestine!

While wading we were accompanied by groups of Arab women, shepherdesses veiled in dark blue, graceful and beautiful in shape, with jars on their heads. And sheep and goats, and cows swollen with milk, and hundreds of calves. Abundance now and pastoral calm. After the desert, the Promised Land.

❖ ❖ ❖

CONTINUING FOR A long time yet in the velvety barley fields. Not a tree, not even any bushes. Nothing but cultivated green everywhere.

And the countryside has more and more people. All around there are laborers in burnouses who are working this rich and fertile soil, riddled with countless furrows. It looks somewhat like La Beauce or certain parts of Normandy. Only instead of villages, we see Arab camps: long shaggy tents hugging the wet grass and pitched one behind the other. They seem to be processions of huge black caterpillars against a very green background.

This worked soil bristles with men and animals that live off it, cultivate it, and deplete it. Our eyes are still glazed by images of wastelands, and the soil gives the impression of a moth-eaten fur or an expensive rug chewed by worms.

❖ ❖ ❖

CAMP TONIGHT ON damp grass and under a gray sky, surrounded by the immense barley fields of Canaan.

We are near a very rich tribe, whose sheik comes right away to my tent and invites me to dinner in his. He is strikingly handsome, with an eagle-beak nose and big wide eyes full of warmth. His veil of silk lamé with multicolored stripes is held on his forehead by cording of gold. He wears two burnouses, one on top of the other, one black, the other white, which he bears with royal grace.

I accept only to have the traditional coffee in his tent. I go there at the time of the setting sun, accompanied by Sheiks Hassan and Aït, who have become my faithful companions.

It's a bit far in the cold evening wind. And the green plain is turning gold from the shiny surfaces of the plantings, a shade of gold that is paler and more northern than that of the desert.

His tent for receiving company is made of camelskin, like all those in his tribe, and is open wide to the countryside. It is unfurnished, with only a few beautiful weapons hanging here and there. He has me sit near him on a rug. His two brothers then beside us. Then the young Sheik of Petra, then his cousin Aït. And they light a fire of branches in the dirt, to prepare our coffee.

One by one a lot of other people begin to arrive. After they have touched my hand, they hunker down around us and form a silent assembly. They are notables of the tribe, severely coiffed with Meccan veils, mostly old men with handsome heads framed by white beards.

And over this row of majestic faces, one can see the distant circle of the plain, the endless green barley, the caterpillaring of countless tents along the west horizon, and the parade of herds coming in, sheep that bleat in tight bunches, cattle that low, calves that leap, and herd dogs busily yapping. These are the riches of our superb host, passing before our eyes in the dying sunlight, in a last golden ray.

This is a pastoral tribe. This sheik possesses all the surrounding territories, far beyond what you can see. He tells us that he moves his camp every month. The coffee is being served in very small cups, and he confides that he has just spent two years as a captive in Turkish prisons for theft and banditry.

He had often heard of the awesome Jahl family that controls, through cousins or brothers, the entire Petraean desert and the entire land of Edom. But he had never met any of the family personally. He shows his deference to Hassan and questions him intently about the battles of Kerak, the arrival of Turkish soldiers from Damascus, and all the recent desert events. And Hassan takes on princely airs that I didn't know he had in him. He relates to the amazed assembly that every year after Ramadan, his father Mohammed-Jahl and a large caravan travel for twelve days to Cairo, where the Khedive never fails to give him two hundred sacks of barley along with a hundred pounds of gold.

❖ ❖ ❖

UPON LEAVING, AND not to be outdone by the handsome sheik, I invite him and his brothers to our evening watch, for coffee in my tent this time.

THIRTY-SEVEN

❖ ❖ ❖ *Saturday, March 24*

WAKE UP LIKE YESTERDAY to the song of larks. We are about twenty kilometers from Gaza and we will arrive by noon. Our entire Bedouin escort will leave us as soon as we have been delivered to the city. There we will get horses to continue our trip to Jerusalem. So this morning is the last time we will ride our camels and travel with our friends from Petra. Moreover our caravan, our dark harnesses, our clothing of neutral colors—all seem to take on a primitive and different look amidst all this green. We no longer blend with our surroundings. The very numerous people who pass us on the streets are dressed in much livelier colors, inspired by the meadows of Canaan, and they ride horses harnessed in red, blue, or yellow. But we are conspicuous by virtue of how high our imposing saddles are in comparison. And their mounts seem like little animals, with rather frivolous and undisciplined gaits. These passersby stare at us and consider us to be strangers from the extreme south.

It takes us a long time to accustom ourselves to this bucolic activity, to these divisions of fertile soil, and to this congestion of life. In the desert we were kings, having limitless expanses at our disposal. Here you must follow narrow paths, where you often have to move aside to let others pass. Here everything is shrunken in dimmer light. And these farmers, as simple as they may seem compared with Western man, are already adept at a thousand niceties of civilization that are unknown to the lazy and free Bedouin, who are experts only in pillage and war.

As for our camels, they react in their own way to the change of scene. Overexcited by this Eden for grazing animals, their gait becomes erratic, they stick their noses into the wind, sniffing the fields and flowers right and left, stopping often with grunts of craving, in order to try reaping a harvest of fresh barley. And they should be

told the warnings of the prophet: "Thou art a swift dromedary tra-
versing her ways; a wild ass used to the wilderness, that snuffeth up
the wind at her pleasure" (*Jeremiah* 11:23–24).

❖ ❖ ❖

THE ARAB ENCAMPMENTS, these camelskin villages, are more numerous than yesterday. Here and there they crown higher ground that
seems bare and almost moth-eaten compared to these endless barley fields, with their beautiful green plush. All the camps are the
same, with their black and hairy dwellings spreading out like
branches. One could say more than ever that these are nests of giant
caterpillars and that they will be devoured by the greenery all
around them . . .

❖ ❖ ❖

AFTER THREE HOURS of travel, the terrain gets more hilly and suddenly: Trees! The first ones! A whole dale of trees. And there is the
sea, which appears as just a line along the horizon. And finally
Gaza, with its houses of gray earth and its white minarets. Gaza, set
with gardens and woods. Gaza almost sumptuous to us simple
desert folk. Gaza suddenly representing security, comfort, commu-
nication with the rest of the world and all the forgotten modern
things . . .

❖ ❖ ❖

IT IS SURPRISING to see annual trees leafless when we consider the illusion of summer that a hotter southern sun had given us. However, the fact is that it is still winter!

For at least half an hour, we move along sandy sunken pathways between hedges of cactus enclosing Edenlike yards full of fig
trees, orange trees, lemon trees, and roses.

Here we see people of white complexion, much less suntanned than we are. A few Christian, Maronite, or Greek ladies, whose raised veils do not hide their features and who are of a startling pink and fresh beauty. Arab women, too, who show only their wide eyes. And Arabs, Turks, and Jews, each group retaining the clothing of its race; this makes a splash and diversity of color that delight the eye when compared with the monotonous gray tones we have just left behind.

At the edge of the city, a loud joyous noise of women's voices. It's a group of washerwomen, whose beautiful bare arms are twisting laundry in running water.

Now we enter the labyrinth of little streets, lined with dwellings that have earthen walls and earthen roofs, on which flowers grow as they do in yards.

From our vantage point high on large desert animals (they are nervous because the houses are so close and they flinch at the least noise of an opened door or closed shutter), we almost pass over these molehill houses, glancing down into small courtyards where women are sitting.

After the dark expressions of the nomads, the faces here seem open, hospitable, and kind. Almost none of the women wear veils. They are beautiful and white, with very dark eyebrows and pink cheeks.

Once we have crossed the city, we find our camp pitched in an Arab cemetery. It is near a spring, and we think it's a bit too close to the dead. But finally this place, designed by the authorities, is, so it seems, the one where all visitors of distinction camp. And our camels kneel for the last time here, dragging their black fringes on the grassy graves. That's it, we will not mount these slow and temperamental creatures again.

We are immediately attacked by a legion of young Israelites, holding out oranges, lemons, old coins, and carnelians engraved with effigies of ancient gods. Most are wearing long oriental robes, but two or three—alas!—have hideous little gray "outfits."

And our Syrian servants arrive to besiege us with pompous welcomes, congratulating us for having survived Bedouin and other desert dangers. A speech is made by the one of the three servants who had been the most afraid on the road . . . For their trouble we give them as a gift a chest that thoughtful friends had obliged us to bring from Cairo and that we have never even opened. (It contains bandages for wounds and drugs for fever and the poison of scorpions and snakes.)

Then we dispose of our useless rifles, which did nothing more than kill the poor owl at Oued-Gherafeh. It was as easy as a stroll to cross the desert!

However, it is undeniable that we feel a little letdown now. It seems we have shaken off and thrown away from our shoulders something like a cloak of lead. We are very pleased to hold again a thousand little modern inventions, not very pretty, it is true, but rather convenient when you are used to them. We are as delighted by the availability of postal service and telegraph as our camels were to find green barley this morning . . .

❖   ❖   ❖

THE OTTOMAN GOVERNOR of Gaza is the first person we visit. He is a likable and distinguished prince, the seventeenth son of the famous pasha Beder-Khan, prince of Kurdistan, who was for many years in conflict with the government of Constantinople. He lives in the higher part of the city and has a stone house in the Turkish style. In his neighborhood other houses like his are municipal buildings and the residences of military authorities. Some telegraph lines head toward Jerusalem across these tailored properties. But the rest of the city, except the mosques and fountains, is constructed of sun-dried earth, like the little houses in the southern oases.

First thing, we are surprised that Gaza, so near the desert, doesn't have any walls for defense against Bedouin attacks. The explanation given is that its inhabitants are themselves "half-marauders, half-receivers of stolen goods, whom the Bedouin find it useful to appease." In addition all the nomads from the surrounding territories come to the bazaars of Gaza to shop.

❖ ❖ ❖

AND TODAY WE ACT like the nomads. We have just left the deep Desert of Pharan and have practically nothing left. So in the dark and crowded alleys of the bazaars, we finish our day buying outfits, shoes, and harnesses. Indeed we cannot continue our journey dressed as Bedouin, especially since we no longer have camels. Nor can we put on our European clothes, because we had shipped our trunks to Jerusalem by sea. And this change of clothing amuses us. Our eyes have been numbed by the desert, and we are struck with the beautiful colors of the Palestinian robes and burnouses . . . In the alley of the Turkish slippermakers, we bump into Hassan and Aït, who are buying red Moroccan leather boots with metal on the heels for crushing snakes. One of their men accompanies them, carrying their previous purchases in his arms. For their camels they have bought head ornaments decorated with glass beads and shells. We join them to continue our shopping together, like a band of excited children dazzled by all the shiny things in these stalls.

Night is falling when we come back to our tents in the cemetery, loaded down with impressive frivolous things.

In front of our camp are hills bristling with graves. Our camels are grazing there in the increasing darkness.

And behind us is the city, whose minarets, in honor of Ramadan, all light up with a crown of fire.

❖ ❖ ❖

THE SKY FILLS with stars. And westward the zodiacal light traces out a persistent slash of phosphorus. Instead of our accustomed desert silence, we have here a very noisy Ramadan night. Until morning we hear the racket of music and voices, religious songs, and rolling of drums. At times you could think they were squads of crazed muezzins saying prayers together in high-pitched and depressing tones. Groups of carolers come by lantern light to go around the cemetery where we are, using tambourines that beat out ancient Arab rhythms. And also there is the steady barking of stray dogs, endless concerts of frogs in the marshes, and, during a few quiet pauses, the distant lapping of the sea.

THIRTY-EIGHT

❖❖❖ *Sunday, March 25 Easter Sunday*

G AZA, ONE OF THE oldest cities in the world and already named in the Bible during the shadowy epochs before Abraham (*Genesis* x:19). Gaza was taken and retaken, destroyed and rebuilt by the ancient peoples of the earth. The Egyptians took it twenty times. It has also belonged to the Philistines, to the *giants of the race of Anakims* (*Joshua* xi:21–22), to the Assyrians, the Greeks, the Romans, the Arabs, and the Crusaders. Its deep soil is loaded with ruins and is full of bones and treasures. The earthen hill that supports the city is an artificial hill, resting on masonry constructed in the dim and distant past. All around it are tunnels of all ages, leading heaven knows where. Its countryside is riddled with bottomless pits, where lizards and snakes dwell.

At several moments in history, it was splendid, especially in the time of the god Marnas, who had a famous temple there. Today the sands have blocked its port and crumbled its marble. It is just a humble market at the edge of the desert, where caravans buy provisions.

Its appearance has remained Saracen. Above the dilapidated pile of its houses rise mosques and funerary kiosks with white cupolas, and above them rise slim palm trees and huge sycamores.

A land of ruins and dust. Whole neighborhoods of clay or dried earth, and here and there lie an old piece of Saracen marble, a shield of the Crusades, a piece of an ancient column, a saint or a Baal. Pieces of temples pave the streets. Friezes of Greek palaces on the ground in front of doorways.

Few people walking, and of course, no sign of carriages. Instead one sees camels, horses, and donkey colts.

A few white and green turbans sitting on the steps of the places of worship. All the activity is in the dark bazaar, covered with faded palm leaves, where Bedouin from different desert tribes use their bandit money to buy camel harnesses, saber scabbards, barley, and dates.

❖ ❖ ❖

IN A MOST HOLY mosque is the tomb of Nebi-el-Hachem, grandfather of Mohammed and current patron of the city.

On this bright sunlit Easter morning, we go in. First there is a vast courtyard, surrounded with white arcades. Some men are there praying, but above all it is filled with very young children, who are playing under the great blue sky. In the East this is the custom: the yards and courtyards of the mosques are the places for babies to gather. Their innocent little games are considered natural and appropriate, and they play alongside prone old men in prayer.

The youngest children, those who can scarcely run, have bracelets of bells on their ankles. This is so that their mothers can hear where they are, just as one puts bells on goats in the fields.

Through several pointed arches closed with wrought-iron doors, this courtyard leads to quiet enclosures, where a high luxuriant spring grass is shaded by palm trees. These must be places where the dead sleep.

The saint's tomb is at one of the corners. The thick door, decorated with ancient sculptures, is locked with a key. Someone who was praying there goes to get the old watchman priest, and we sit down, surrounded by religious peace, to wait in the shade of the white arches.

He arrives slowly. He is a priest with a white beard and a green turban. He turns the key, and we go in. Under a grim little cupola, fretted on top, painted with arabesques whose color has been faded by humidity and rain, is the large catafalque of green cloth. At the four corners are some copper spheres crowned with crescents, and above it all is the dead man's turban, veiled by faded gauze.

❖ ❖ ❖

PEOPLE COME AND go along the little streets and bazaars. They are busy with their daily lives. This is neither Sunday nor Easter for them, but rather any day of the calendar—and in this first city of Judea, nothing elicits for us the memory of Christ.

However, here is a larger mosque, whose Gothic door looks like a cathedral portal. The threshold where we take off our slippers is like the threshold of a church. Inside there is a large nave in the form of a Latin cross, with columns of gray marble. Here and there on the walls are more crosses, which have obviously been removed, but whose impressions still persist under layers of whitewash. A church in effect, built by Crusaders of burning faith, who once came and perished on holy ground. What power they had, and what marvels they were able to accomplish! How much more beautiful their church was because it was built in wartime on foreign soil! And how surprising to find it still standing! . . .

In its placid whiteness, lit by reflections of the great Easter sun that illuminates it inside, something Christian still survives . . . The Franks who built it seven centuries ago had already confused the Jesus of the Bible with childish legends—and now, to top it all, the dark green flags of Mohammed occupy the ravaged nave, taking the place of images the naive Crusaders had erected. But that's all right, something of the Savior is here, something almost nothing and infinitely sweet—with a vague hint today of Sunday celebration, of Easter celebration . . .

The Crusaders have left their traces here everywhere. And one would risk disturbing their bones if one dug into this old soil laden with debris and the dead. The Turkish citadel, begun in the thirteenth century, then remodeled and changed in every epoch of history, offers on its walls a mixture of delicate Saracen fretwork and heavy chivalric shields; on them grow lichens now, the plants of ruins.

❖ ❖ ❖

IN A HIGHER QUARTER, we stop at a spot where one can see all of Gaza gray with earthen houses, its few minarets and its few whitened domes ringed with palm trees. Then the remains of its ramparts from some past epoch. Their layout is no longer apparent, and they disappear into cemeteries. A whole world, these cemeteries reaching out into the countryside. In one of them under a sycamore, a group of women wail loudly for a dead one according to official ritual, and their chanted lament rises up to us. Many beautiful shaded yards, many paths lined with cactus. Rows of donkeys are using the paths to carry skins of water down to the city. And finally the distant sea, the velvet of barley, and the desert sands. A great mournful panorama to which it is difficult to assign a time in history. And over there, covered with tombs, the lonely hill where Samson, leaving the courtesan's tent one night, went and removed the portals of Gaza from the Philistines (*Judges* xvi:2-3).

❖ ❖ ❖

WHEN WE GET BACK to camp around noon, there is quite a bit of activity around it. Some Jewish merchants of antique objects are waiting for us, sitting on the tombs. Some Greek Christians, all dressed up, and some of whom are wearing European suits, are also watching for our return.

Later the inquisitive and the merchants depart, weary, and we are alone. Our Bedouin, who leave this evening for their desert, are asleep, stretched out in the grass. Gaza, now quiet, is resting from the night's festivities. A blistering sun flashes its beams on our white tents. The stones all around are covered with chameleons and lizards.

❖ ❖ ❖

A PEACEFUL AND meditative Easter afternoon. We spend it sitting in front of our tents in these cemeteries, watching the comings and goings of lizards, who come out of the ground in ever-increasing numbers. On the warm tombstones of the graves, they chase each

other and play. At the edges of the graves, there are two or three
that rise way up on their legs and waddle strangely along.

The air becomes thick, thick. The air turns dark without visible clouds. The sun, dull and yellow suddenly, no longer sheds
light and seems to be dying. Its disk is sharp and lacking rays, as if
seen through smoked glass. And one could say that the end of the
world is near.—A khamsin blast will pass, and the neighboring
deserts will sweep over us . . .

In the sudden storm, a strong wind comes up, bringing whirlwinds of sand and dust . . . "The burden of the desert of the sea. As
whirlwinds in the south pass through; so it cometh from the desert,
from a *terrible land.*" (*Isaiah* xxi:1).

❖ ❖ ❖

BY EVENING THE dry storm is calm, and strollers reappear. We receive the visit of the city's governor, the likable Kurdish prince, and
a few Moslem priests. Then our saddle horses and our pack mules,
ordered from Jerusalem yesterday by telegram, arrive exhausted
from the forced march and fall over on their sides like foundered
animals. Along the cactus-lined paths, the herds are coming back to
the city from the countryside, and night falls.

Around midnight, when the moon is high, our Bedouin are to
leave for Petra, taking with them the Turkish officer and two soldiers who had accompanied us. In the twilight they group their
camels and fetter them. Then they light big fires to cook the
farewell meal.

And we exchange friendly good-byes. We embrace Sheiks
Hassan and Aït, and we exchange gifts with them. Hassan gives me
his dagger, and I give him my revolver.

❖ ❖ ❖

THE NIGHT HAD been very dark, and here in the cemetery we were in
a kind of gloomy chaos, where nothing could be seen.

But now is the time for moonrise. Behind us the city, which we had lost sight of, begins to emerge in black silhouette on an irregular blood-red fire looming on the horizon. Then the fire condenses into a mass of red fire, ever rounder, into a rising globe that suddenly turns white, the way coals burst into flame without warning. It lights us more and more. It is a disk of silvery fire now that rises radiant and floating, and that fills the sky with light . . . And on this shining background, minarets stand out, and palm trees sketch their delicate black plumes. Everything that seemingly did not exist a short time ago is reborn, a thousand times more magical than in daylight, transfigured into a great oriental fairyland . . . Also the tiers of cemeteries all around us gradually appear. A muted light, somewhat pink, that was born on the tops of the tombs, continues to expand and spread while coming down, like a long obtrusive stain, then finally falls onto the lower ground where we are: just a bunch of nomads, of people and animals, around dying fires . . . And then we can see perfectly in the beautiful blazing light of the moon! . . .

❖ ❖ ❖

THE MOON IS HIGH. It is time for the Bedouin to leave. And now the silent file of their camels begins, in rays of pink silver. From the high backs of their swaying mounts, Sheiks Hassan and Aït send us a last wave of friendship as they go by. They are returning to the *terrible land* of their birth, where they like to live—and their departure seals our desert dream.

Tomorrow morning at dawn we set off for Jerusalem! . . .